Sue Schell

A Simplicity Revolution

Finding Happiness in the New Reality

iUniverse, Inc.
Bloomington

A Simplicity Revolution
Finding Happiness in the New Reality

iUniverse books may be ordered through booksellers or by contacting:

*iUniverse
1663 Liberty Drive
Bloomington, IN 47403
www.iuniverse.com
1-800-Authors (1-800-288-4677)*

ISBN: 978-1-4620-2386-8 (sc)
ISBN: 978-1-4620-2387-5 (e)

Library of Congress Control Number: 2011910074

Printed in the United States of America

iUniverse rev. date: 8/10/2011

To my loving and supportive husband, Tim, and son, Alex, who enrich and simplify my life in countless ways.

"What we plant in the soil of contemplation, we shall reap in the harvest of action."

—Meister Eckhart

Foreword

By Professor Robert Launay,
Northwestern University (PhD, Cambridge, 1975).
Dr. Robert Launay is a social/cultural anthropologist trained in the
United States, England, and France.

Sometime, somehow, this nation has lost its bearings. Even before the financial meltdown of 2008 and the recession it brought in its wake, many Americans were convinced of this. Now, it has become all more patently apparent.

A hundred years ago, the great French sociologist Emile Durkheim coined a word for this: anomie. Anomie is the sinking feeling that the rules and patterns that guided your life suddenly cease to work. It is the awful void we feel when a loved one dies, when a relationship breaks up, when we are laid off, or, for many of us, when we retire. Durkheim suggested that anomie could explain certain regular patterns in suicide rates. But anomie does not just affect individuals. Whole societies, too, can succumb to anomie, when their core values cease to give meaning to the lives of their members.

One common reaction to such a situation is to want to

turn back the clock, to return to the "good old days" and the values that used to sustain us and that, presumably, we have lost. This kind of nostalgia is nothing new. In the early days of the Roman Empire, moralists and historians, like Livy, Tacitus, and Plutarch, lamented the loss of the virtues that presumably characterized the early days of the Roman Republic. Unfortunately, the past that we long for is generally a mythical creation, an idealized version that never existed at the time. The love of nature and the countryside is a product of modern industrial society; agrarian societies are entirely unsentimental about nature. There is no way we can return to the America of the founding fathers, no matter how much we would like to. There is no point asking what kind of car they would drive. (For the record, however, George Washington sent an army against those who refused to pay taxes during the Whiskey Rebellion; partisans of the Tea Party movement might want to think twice before choosing their heroes.)

The challenges we are facing are new, and so the solutions and the values that we forge to meet them must also be new, however much we can still take inspiration from the past. We must, in order to confront our national malaise, identify its roots. Here, Sue Schell has hit the nail on the head. We are, more than ever, an addicted society. Drugs, of course, are not the only problem (though that problem is real enough); we are, as she says, addicted to "stuff." We can see the evidence easily enough in daily life. Drivers have their ears glued to their cell phones, in flagrant violation of the law. When I am behind the wheel, I find that I must increasingly pay attention to pedestrians crossing the street while texting, totally oblivious to their surroundings. Cars, guns, video games, gambling, fast food, soft drinks, Twitter—the list goes on and on.

In the struggle for values, our national mythology seems to give the edge to the rugged individualists. Our national hero is the cowboy, the rugged loner in the fight for truth, justice, and the American way. This is, of course, a highly idealized vision of our past. The West was won, not by cowboys, but by railway companies who extended their empire on the backs of Chinese and Irish workers so desperate to escape starvation at home that they were prepared to accept any work overseas under the most degrading and inhuman conditions imaginable. It is no accident that corporations still use the myth of the cowboy to market their addictive merchandise. Why is the Marlboro man the most iconic emblem of cigarettes? What could be more cowboyish than our passion, not only for guns, but for video games that turn us into ersatz gunslingers? Why do SUVs—the biggest, meanest, most fuel-inefficient vehicles on the road—almost always have no passengers beside the driver? Shouldn't SUV stand for Single User Vehicle?

Sue Schell shows us that we have to get rid of the cowboy, that we need to enshrine the virtues of simplicity, and that, most of all, we can be individuals without being "individualists." As smoking bans have shown us, only the mobilization of public opinion in favor of government that serves the public good rather than private interests can cure us of our addictions and point to a better way for us to live our lives. For example, if we had cheap, efficient, and broadly available public transportation, we could wean ourselves off our addiction to gas-guzzling cars. If we had more equitable distribution of income, the poor might not consider gambling their only hope, however illusory and remote, of living a decent life. If teachers were better paid and class sizes were smaller, not only would the dismal quality of American public education improve, but teaching itself would be an attractive and available career for the best and the brightest. Simplicity, as Sue Schell envisions it, is not simply a program for making our lives better as individuals—though of course there is nothing wrong with that, on the contrary! But *A Simplicity Revolution*, if it is to work, must be a social revolution, a way to guide ourselves, not only as individuals, but as a society.

Table of Contents

Introduction

Never doubt that a small group of thoughtful
committed people can change the world.
Indeed, it is the only thing that ever has.
                                    —Margaret Mead

In order for *A Simplicity Revolution* to work in America, it will have to be viewed as a social revolution, a way to guide ourselves—not only as individuals, but as a society. Today, we find ourselves living in a celebrity-driven culture that is missing one essential thing. We are losing our ability to look beyond the superficial and extraneous. Suffice it to say, every day we are influenced by our environment and by what we see going on around us. In our society, those greedy and acquisitive sorts of individuals, who are often treated as heroes in the media, have concerned me. The way we have matured as a nation somehow hasn't felt healthy this last decade. I'm referring to how disposable we treat relationships, nature, clothing, and all of the "too much stuff" we collect in our lives. Personally, I think it's time for a new way of thinking in America!

As an activist, I needed to write about how socially destructive the last few decades have been for our country. When I read Jared Diamond's 2005 book, *Collapse: How Societies Choose to Fail or Succeed,* I couldn't help but relate to the fact that, given this serious juncture at which we find our nation, we could possibly be making choices right now that will determine whether our country continues growing in a positive fashion or fails to adapt to the new global world order.

It is my plan to address these societal issues that are happening before us in America. Issues such as how we address our climate change problems and our battle to keep our national education system strong are matters that will have a long-term, far-reaching impact on America. In fact, in order for a Simplicity Revolution to be successful, our American society will need to unite in an attempt to let go of several cultural bad habits that we've acquired. For example, this culture of supersizing everything we eat and own, although once embraced, needs to be cut loose.

While the thought of driving a beastly Hummer down the highway in 1997 might have been appealing to some, by 2007 it started to become a joke. That is when I knew there was hope for us. In fact, when a person needlessly drives any oversized vehicle, the owner is doing nothing more than wasting his money (and gas) and showing a disregard for our immediate environment as well as our planet.

I believe America's "go big or go home" attitude led to many of America's current problems—for example, how much we eat. This has led to America becoming home to the most obese people in the world. According to the CDC, within the past twenty years, obesity in adults has increased by 60 percent and has tripled in the past thirty years for children. Thirty-three percent of all Americans are obese, and obesity-related deaths have reached more than 300,000 a year. No wonder that we needed to have bigger vehicles. In fact, SUVs were put into use just to go to our local grocery stores and other local destinations, and we also had to build those huge McMansions, even if we couldn't afford them.

So as our economy was going down the drain, I began seeing an explosive thirst for simplicity all around me, which is why I felt compelled to write this book. I don't want to be too dramatic, but I was seeing, hearing, and feeling America aching for a simpler lifestyle. First, I witnessed it from within my own inner circle of friends and then in people I would meet at the library, at the grocery store, and on the Internet. People were looking for more in their life after becoming disgusted with their own overextended lives. People were recognizing that there was more to life than working hard for the money, only to be spending it as fast as it came in. I believe—or, at least, I want to believe—that people were recognizing that having their life rooted in relationships and not just purchased "stuff" was a much more fulfilling way to live. It was as if you could almost hear people calling out, "Enough already!"

After millions of people lost their jobs—and then some, ultimately, their homes—our country moved into a heightened state of anxiety over the possibility that

America's best days could be behind us. Was the American dream now in jeopardy?

Notably, people began turning their backs on excessive consumption in search of something less costly yet satisfying. But besides the job and income loss, there appeared to be something more happening here. That preoccupation with consumerism and brands was being reprioritized. Certainly, America's real challenge for the future will come in confronting its political polarization and dysfunction head-on! This will require our society as a whole to place value on simplicity much more than it has in the recent past.

Over the last several decades, in our celebrity-driven and influenced culture, the frenzy of needing this and buying that had become insanity. This resulted in a personal debt implosion, which probably doesn't need much explaining. Entire generations of consumers grew up with the idea of instant gratification and, thus, the American credit culture developed. Since the popularization of the installment loan to buy cars, home appliances, and just about anything else, the idea of saving to buy something has nearly disappeared from the American financial vocabulary.

This book is a commentary on America's boom-and-bust decade and the "corporatocracy" that caused it. It is meant to be a wake-up call regarding some of our overconsumption, unsustainable tendencies. As became apparent, some of the recent pain in our country resulted from Americans' desires to supersize their lives more than warranted by their paychecks. After millions of people lost their jobs and then their homes, our country began facing anxiety over the possibility that America's best days may be behind us. Then again, America getting hit by the worst banking crisis in U.S. history since the Great Depression felt like a flashback to a time in our country's history that we never thought possible again. We had grown to assume that our banks, our investment houses, and our very own government were just too big to fail. But to our amazement, some of them did fail.

Chapters—such as "Four Guideposts to a Simpler Life," "Why Fiscal Discipline Is Like a Physical Fitness Routine," and "For Happiness that Lasts, Try This!"— will offer tips on avoiding the scary situations that many people found themselves in during this latest economic downturn. The situation I refer to is that of being a hamster trapped on a wheel in a cage with no means of escape, which is another way of describing the debt treadmill. It's amazing how improved a person's quality of life can be, just by simplifying some of our daily lifestyle habits and thereby avoiding stressful situations.

Living a simple life means a lot more than knowing how to live frugally. It is about living an authentic life that lets you exist in the kind of life you dream of living—the sort of life that provides you time for self-reflection and is not measured by materialistic goods. I began seeing people, from coast to coast, in big cities to small towns, longing for simpler lifestyles that were once again rooted in relationships and not just the "stuff" that can be purchased. I believe that a simpler lifestyle will eventually prove to be the silver lining found in this Great Recession.

I have to admit that writing about America's loss of

confidence in the American Dream is painful for me, because it feels like losing a part of our history. Hollywood has always captured the American story so well in its films. From the time when moviemaking first began in the 1920s to the present, America has been portrayed as this sovereign land of opportunity. The world became familiar with our American culture through seeing it acted out in film and reading about it in books. One thing was certain: the American dream was there for the taking by anyone willing to work hard. In America, anything was possible, and thus we became the recipient of immigrants from across the world.

And personally speaking, it has meant so much in my life because I lived it! The American dream has represented, and always will represent, America at its finest. It illustrates the freedom that everyone in this country can enjoy under our democratic form of government. In America, anyone really could reach for the stars because … this is America! And that is the sort of sentiment that I hope will always be available to the generations that follow.

People tend to think of the word "revolution" as it pertains to politics. But it is my intent to use it to provoke and describe the cultural changes happening in our country today. There will be a little bit of politics involved here, because it would be almost impossible to write about this subject without acknowledging some of what is happening on our political front. It is my hope that this book delivers an upbeat message, encouraging Americans to pay attention to their priorities a little more closely and to slow down a little bit. Stop rushing thoughtlessly around from one must-do item to another.

Much of what some people are looking for will not be found in shopping malls. In fact, if you want to get off of that hamster wheel, also known as the debt treadmill, you really need to stay away from those tempting places, because items you don't really need have a way of making it onto your credit card.

Sociologists believe that whenever a society loses its equilibrium, next comes a revolution. Throughout history, countries going through prolonged hard economic times, as America currently is, are more likely to see the introduction of new cultural traditions and ideas, which is what this Simplicity Revolution is all about. If we can commit to living a new sort of lifestyle, perhaps we can prevent the type of economic disaster we have just lived through from happening again. A Simplicity Revolution emphasizes the importance of interpersonal relationships, positive thinking, and taking time to care about ourselves, our relationships, our families, our government, and our communities. Really, don't you think that these types of commitments could lead to a healthier country in which the pursuit of happiness is possible for more people? And doesn't this sound like something we could all put to use in our own lives and communities—say, tomorrow?

I grew up in a small bungalow in the heart of Chicago. My family was middle class all the way; in fact, I suppose we were really lower middle class, but at the time I certainly didn't recognize the difference.

Once I graduated from the University of Illinois at Chicago with my degree in journalism, I grabbed onto the great American dream, spending the next twenty-five years working in the business world. As a result, there aren't many desk jobs I haven't done. Part of that time, I worked as a news reporter for a Chicago newspaper, a singer, and a horse-racing executive. Next, I worked on legislative issues for then–Illinois Governor James Thompson. When I left that job, I became a management consultant and an owner of a small business for five years. Now, I am a writer and a political activist. Just ask me someday and I'll be happy to relate some of the crazy things I've seen and done. These experiences helped me grow as an individual, become more actively engaged in my community, and build a family life rich in the values I learned in the process.

It is probably because I lived the great American Dream that I strongly believe everyone should have an opportunity in life to lift themselves up through hard work. A person needs to be able to aspire toward a better, more fulfilling life. When a person has to go to work every day feeling like he doesn't have any choices or opportunities to better himself, it can begin to drag not only him down, but our society as well. This is just one reason that I believe keeping the American Dream alive is crucial to the health of our nation.

Times are hard now and, like me, you probably know people who have lost jobs. Many people are hurting from the stress of trying to balance the many demands on their lives: the fast pace, the need to constantly either be looking for work or multitasking to cover the work of two or three people in their current jobs. Home foreclosures are causing unimaginable pain in so many people's lives, decimating blocks, neighborhoods, and, by extension, entire cities. Overall, there are more financial pressures than ever, and yet, many of these financial pressures were avoidable. Wouldn't it have been simpler to live without some of the "stuff" that helped get us into these stressful predicaments?

The first decade of the 2000s was remarkable for many different reasons. It began with a series of busts (from the dot-com bubble to the Enron scandal) and closed with a series of busts (from financial systems to the auto industry), but sandwiched in the middle were some serious booms (the housing market and stock market). Many economists are predicting this first decade of the twenty-first century will become known as America's lost decade, but I disagree. I much prefer to think that this time in history will become known for when America soured on its "supersize me" lifestyles. We began living more principled, sustainable lifestyles. This resulted in huge cultural changes that started slowly, but as the economy declined and the average American's lifestyle came down with it, the Simplicity Revolution started gaining momentum, thus altering the pathway many Americans had been taking. It's my hope that once you read the following chapters you will come to agree with me.

On June 7, 2010, a Zogby Interactive survey stated that 22 percent of Americans said their expectations for their career and possessions had decreased. For many of the 22 percent, this was a conscious choice, not a decision forced by bad circumstances. More than one-third of them said they just desired a simpler life. This is greater than the quarter who said they realized they probably would not be able to attain their goal, or the same number who were working at a job that paid less than their previous job and did not expect to ever be as well-off again.

People began turning their backs on excessive consumption in search of something less costly, yet satisfying. People were not simply making do with new personal and national economic realities, but it appeared more was happening here. Apparently, the Zogby survey showed that there was a growing rejection of a lifestyle obsessed with consumption and too often devoid of deeper meaning. America's preoccupation with consumerism and brands was being reprioritized. Most importantly, it sure looked like America was getting back to "basics," and in my opinion, it was none too soon!

I've attempted to fill this book with thought-provoking ideas regarding the cultural need for simplicity in our lives as well as other very serious issues confronting America, such as our declining education system, the disappearing middle class, and our ever-worsening climate issues, all of which will directly be affecting the future of the United States for years to come.

No one claims to want to live a more complicated life. However, our culture has encouraged us to become part of the greatest accumulation nation in the world. Take the baby boomer generation, for example. Some are now coming to the age of retirement and the realization that perhaps they shouldn't have purchased all of that "stuff" they thought they just had to have. What's it worth today? Probably less money than what was originally paid. And now, what are you going to do with all of this "stuff" you thought you had to have? Probably try to unload it at your next garage sale!

You may not agree with everything I have to say in this book, but I hope my words will at least help you think about how you can simplify your life, which really will mean getting back to the basics by exploring ways to make your life more fulfilling and sustainable. Some of this may surprise you and sometimes appear so obvious; you'll think, *I already knew that!* Keep in mind, we all inherently know much of what I'm writing about, but we get distracted by the busyness of our daily lives. It is my sole intention to jog your memory so that you might reflect upon the little things each person can do immediately to begin improving their own life and, thus, help with the sustainability of our planet. After all, we are all really connected and, just as we need so much of what our dear planet offers us, we also have a responsibility to preserve this planet for our beloved progeny.

So why do you need this book? Because it can serve to remind you how you can fine-tune your life and perhaps rediscover or uncover your ability to be happy living a downscaled, simpler life. It can provide you with a refreshing new outlook. I hope to reveal to you that the things in life from which you derive your pleasure are not necessarily "stuff" you purchase. Our greatest pleasure's in life are usually our kids who can drive us crazy some of the time, yet endear themselves to us every day of their lives, or your life partner who is expected home from work soon, or your parents who will be driving 150 miles to visit your family this weekend, and those wonderful friends of yours who at times almost feel like your guardian angels.

Over the last few years, I've seen more and more

people desire a simpler and more meaningful lifestyle. Most people think of the American Dream relating to material "stuff." However, I think it should be thought of as having the ability to obtain personal fulfillment, a simpler life that includes hobbies, volunteering, and, perhaps most importantly, finding that elusive "quality time" with family and friends.

In these changing times, I recommend you read the words of author and philosopher Meister Eckhart. One of my favorite quotations of Eckhart is: "People should think less about what they ought to do and more about what they ought to be." I say yes to that! Too many of us tend to try to go with the flow, which is not always a naturally good fit for the type of life we may actually desire to live. Sometimes in order to be true to ourselves, going against the flow may feel more natural and allow you to be yourself. In order to live a true life, you need to spend time being honest with yourself. Take time for personal reflection, whether in the form of a silent meditation or a walking meditation outside or inside. This time of quiet contemplation may allow you to find answers to questions regarding your personal life path choices. And always remember, nothing has to be forever. If you enter into one thing and find it is the wrong choice, revisit your choices and begin to reexamine your likes and dislikes. In due course, you will be rewarded with peace of mind. We are all capable of reaching a more focused state of mind, but only when we find and take the time to quietly think without all of the interferences and distractions of the world fighting for our attention. I hope you will benefit from my own journey, which required opening my eyes to the fact that a simpler life provided me with an inner sense of well-being. That frenzy of needing this and buying that had produced chaos in my life. I also was tired of thinking that I needed to be the vice president of an organization or had to have the type of job that declared to the world that I was smart, able, and worthy, regardless of whether I found true satisfaction from the work. After doing some inner soul searching regarding who I wanted to be in life, I realized that I no longer needed to prove anything to anyone allowing me to openly say, I am a writer. This required me to accept that I would be working for far less money, but the trade-off—a huge amount of inner wealth.

Since becoming a writer, I have learned something important that I would now like to share with you. A way to determine whether you are in the right job—by that I mean a job that you believe is what you are—and a job that is meant for you is to examine your life in the way I have.

I admit it! In most of my previous jobs I was an unabashed clock watcher. Sitting in meetings or presentations, I always was glancing down at my watch to see how much more time was left until it was over. Now mind you, some of these were extremely important meetings. For instance, sitting next to the governor should have required undivided attention. But what I now know is that when you are fully engaged, loving, and invested in your work, hours can go by like minutes, so much so that at times I have lost track of time while writing this book. I have heard the birds singing outside my office window, as if calling out to me to begin my gardening, yet I cannot leave my work. And I know it is because I have finally found my life's work. This is why I now look at simplicity as a form of cleansing. I welcome a Simplicity Revolution with open arms!

Having to shed a culture of entitlement is not an easy hurdle to get over. No longer can we Americans afford to assume that our economic growth will always continue. Now we're just wondering, *What the heck happened, and how do we get out of this mess?* The Great Recession is definitely going to leave a lasting impression on many of us for years to come. The questions really are: What lessons can we take away from this? Will it change America's voracious appetite for always needing to have more and the best? Will we have learned that living beyond our means is simply unsustainable? The Great Recession supposedly ended in 2009, yet it has left behind a generation that is living in poverty and, in some cases, even on the streets. The government considers a family of four to be impoverished if it takes in less than $22,000 a year. Based on a March 6, 2011, broadcast on *60 Minutes*, our government's projections of unemployment estimate the poverty rate for kids in this country will soon hit 25 percent. Those children would be the largest American generation to be raised in such hard times since the Great Depression.

Does the need for simplicity apply to the poor? It sure does, but in a different way. A Simplicity Revolution really is a middle-class social movement, because it concerns making a choice about how to live, and the poor have very few choices. In fact, that applies to more and more of the dwindling middle class, as well. Instead of cutting back on their spending, the poor need more money to spend. They need policies that support higher minimum wages, affordable housing, and health-care policies that simply allow the poor to live a less complicated and less stressful life.

The answer is clear. Americans have to produce a new "bootstrap" generation, one capable of pulling itself up through this incredibly difficult time and creating a better, easier world to live in than the one it now has to deal with. Finding good-paying jobs will be more difficult in the foreseeable future; staying out of debt will be even harder. Americans are going to find that, above and beyond everything else, they need to rediscover the American sense of optimism, which for the first time in my memory is hanging on by only a thread. Yet, with the boom-and-bust decade we have lived through, one has to wonder whether America can regain its strong sense of optimism. I hope this book can inspire everyone to be aware that, even when our wallets may be empty, life can still be beautiful and fulfilling! This is what I believe, and hopefully you too will come to share my outlook and start your efforts to get America back on track.

This probably won't shock you, but throughout history, simplicity in our culture has always had its moments in the sun. One such time was known as the American transcendentalist movement in the mid-1800s, which produced writer Henry David Thoreau, who said, "Following a doctrine of simplicity allows people to live free and opens up new ways of understanding human nature." A Simplicity Revolution really is about you getting your life back and living life with more concentration and focus so that you can actually enjoy living daily life. Being mindful of the quality of your life as well as the lives of those around you is truly a wonderful gift to yourself, family, friends, and neighbors.

A study published on December 4, 2010, in the *British Medical Journal* says happiness can quickly go viral within your social network. Researchers looked at twenty years' worth of data on more than five thousand individuals and found that when any one person was happy, his friends became more likely to share that joy. Benefits spread out to three degrees of separation, meaning a better chance at happiness for not only the friends' friends, but also the friends' friends' friends. But don't go thinking your ten thousand buddies on Facebook will bring you happiness. The researchers found that the strength of the effect dissipates over physical distance, with next-door neighbors and friends living nearby getting the biggest boost. So, as you can see, your own happiness is contagious. And so, in order to live a happier life, surround yourself with happy friends, or at least find friends with happy friends.

Perhaps this painful recession was a necessary interlude on our path to a saner, more fulfilled reality, which leads us directly back to this Simplicity movement. The good news I see coming out of all of these challenging times is that I believe we can once again unleash American ingenuity and creativity, creating new jobs for Americans.

When I was thinking of what to name this book, as chance would have it, I came upon the quote from Margaret Mead that opened this introduction. Ironically, its message seemed completely relevant to the issues currently challenging our country. I will never forget a day back in the mid-1970s. I was a sophomore working on my college newspaper at the University of Illinois, and I received a phone call from the secretary of the famous anthropologist, telling me that Dr. Mead was willing to sit down with me for an interview. I felt so unworthy to even be in her presence, and I always remember with great gratitude that Dr. Mead treated me as a legitimate reporter. When I ran across her famous quotation many years later, I felt as though Margaret Mead was speaking directly to me again, and I realized that I had to write this book. I sincerely hope you will continue with me as we explore a new trend based on the much older truth that, by embracing simplicity, we can live a life of meaning, enjoyment, and more fulfillment that truly reflects and restores the "real" American dream.

* * * * * * * * *

Chapter 1
A Simplicity Revolution: Why Now?

* * * * * * * * *

*I believe we would be happier to have a
personal revolution in our individual lives
and go back to simpler living and more
direct thinking. It is the simple things of
life that make living worthwhile, the sweet
fundamental things.*
— Laura Ingalls Wilder, 1917

Laura Ingalls Wilder's quote really hits home for me.
How could this woman, who settled on land not yet
open for homesteading in what was then Indian Territory
near Independence, Kansas (which was the basis of Ingalls's
novel *Little House on the Prairie*), write so beautifully of
simplicity? Like me, many of you probably grew up reading
her depiction of life on the prairie as a child. Or perhaps
you can recall the TV show *Little House on the Prairie*.
If so, then you are probably extremely touched by her
words. When I think about a homesteader's life, I think,
Ah, the good old days. When life was so very simple! Yet it
was, in all actuality, anything *but* simple! Every single

detail of life that today we take for granted would have been much more difficult. Yet here is Laura Ingalls Wilder calling for a "personal revolution in our individual lives to go back to simpler living and more direct thinking!" How beautiful Laura Ingalls Wilder's words were then, and how impactful they can be on our lives today. Laura, I love that your voice is still heard!

You see, a Simplicity Revolution is a movement that our country is ready for after having gone through the boom-and-bust decade that has just ended and enduring that "coporatocracy" that caused it. In order to be successful, this revolution requires our culture to open itself to changing more than just the clothes we wear. This is about changing our priorities, the things we choose to do for ourselves. For example, how many people bought one of those huge McMansions, knowing that they were biting off more financially than they could chew? How many of us have to take blood pressure medications because we are always hurrying just a little too much or perhaps trying too hard to find enough money to pay our bills at the end of each month? Stress studies have shown that people with heightened anxiety, intense anger, and suppressed anger are more at risk of developing high blood pressure than more relaxed individuals. Always think twice about what is the most sustainable choice for yourself, your family, and our planet. If we are successful in this, then never again should we have to see so many American families losing their homes, as we did in 2010. Now, I do not blame these homeowners entirely, since some banks were approving loans for people who barely had the income to cover their mortgage payments! But this is not about pointing fingers; it's about learning how to avoid some of these mistakes in the future.

By 2008, many of us began coming to the painful realization that our society's value system was eroding (think Enron or Bernie Madoff here, just for starters). Our culture's value system had been knocked off-kilter. Our middle-class American lifestyle was now at stake. And here is the one big reason: When the economy faltered, many people began losing jobs therefore they couldn't afford to pay their monthly mortgages. This, and the irrational exuberance which had pushed up real estate prices in many American cities led in part to the bursting of the housing bubble leading to people owing more money on their mortgage than their home was actually now worth. The very home, which had long been associated with living the American dream, now began feeling more like a nightmare. Listening as new cities reported the increasing number of foreclosures of homes every night on the nightly news all around our country was extremely painful. Then it started happening in my own community of middle-class and wealthy homeowners. This came as a shock. I had always believed that real estate was the safest investment a person could make; in fact; I was raised to believe it. There were so many times my father and I would debate this issue. I can recall telling him that home prices were going up in the area near where we'd purchased our home. He would say, "I didn't know you and Tim were thinking of moving." And I would quickly say, "No, we're not moving, at least in the foreseeable future. But I like seeing how much money we are making on our purchase." My dad would laughingly reply, "Well, I didn't buy my house just as an investment. I bought my home to live in. You can't begin counting your money until your house is sold and the money is in your bank account." Hmm … Finally, fifteen years later, I can understand his point. I would guess that many of you would have agreed with me during that housing boom when prices were soaring, but as of two years ago when we started seeing the economic bust hit and prices began sinking, you might be more inclined to think like my father. Unfortunately, many of us have had to watch as our most precious and serious investment continues to deflate.

At times, hasn't it felt like we have been sliding back into a world of poverty, war, and violence? Many of us, prior to this latest recession, didn't think that Americans might ever have to readjust our expectations for the future. So the American dream was going to be only that? A dream?

Did you know that in 2010 there were over one million homes foreclosed? Economists are predicting that in 2011, nearly the same numbers of homes are expected to be taken back by the lending banks. Economists continue to warn us to prepare for what they are calling America's "new normal." I refer to it as the "new reality."

Regardless of how hard this recession has hit you and/or your family, please know there have been some valuable lessons in it. Learning how to live a lighter lifestyle by going back to simpler living and more direct thinking may ultimately be something you will want to celebrate. Did our American values stray off course during the boom-and-bust times? We now know they did. In many cases we'd developed for ourselves an overly complex lifestyle that now Americans are finding very difficult to sustain. Some people are literally living from one financial catastrophe to the next. For these people simplicity is a necessity. We must keep in mind that there are those who choose simplicity for their lives for a variety of personal reasons, such as spirituality, health, quality time for family and friends, reducing their personal ecological footprint, stress reduction, personal taste, or frugality. And others cite a sociopolitical approach to life, including conservation, social justice, ethnic diversity, and sustainable development. And then we have plenty of people doing it in order to survive. It was for all of these reasons that I found myself writing about our current need for simplicity.

As history has shown, America will eventually regain its equilibrium. I believe we are already seeing it happen. Americans are reassessing what we judge important in our lives. However, when the economy turns around, does anyone really think we will return to living the way we had been?

Begin to Feel Content with Your Life

We live our lives with more technological advances than any generation before. The computerization of so many new ways of doing business, our cell phones that went viral very quickly as well as the Social Networking Programs such as Facebook, Twitter, and My Space. Yet we have also witnessed consequences that most of us were not prepared for, such as these massive job losses. Our lives, ironically, are now more complex than ever. We are challenged constantly to upgrade our knowledge, be in touch with more people than ever, and improve our technological tools. We are busy, hurrying to our next task with little time for reflection. I believe that making life more simple and reconnecting with personal values can give us a greater sense of control over our own lives. This could ease some of our panic, and panicked behavior, as the fast pace of technology and increasingly harsher economic environment gives us a desperate feeling of always lagging behind while still trying to keep up.

Whenever I use the word "simplicity," I'm talking about living a peaceful existence in a cooperative society. That goes for all levels of citizens in this country. I aim to show that all Americans need to care about the welfare of all of its citizens—the rich, middle class, and poor, the old and young, the family and the single individual. We expect other countries to abide by our strict rules of humanitarianism. Let us once again expect the same of our own country!

Let me make this clear. Living a simple life is not about frugality. It is about living a life that allows you time to daily reflect on the life you live. Being mindful of the quality of your life as well as that of the lives around you is a wonderful gift to yourself, family, friends, and neighbors. Your own happiness is contagious to those around you. Simplicity is about taking control of your life and resisting the forces in society that urge you to claw your way to the top, to be a winner regardless of consequences. But being a winner does not necessarily make you happy. In fact, it most likely won't! In this book, I will show you ways to an easier, less complicated, more straightforward, simpler lifestyle. With its enormity and, might I say, mind-boggling complexity, our government surely needs a dose of simplicity, don't you think? And look at the mess our public education system is in. Some simple, sensible changes to the quality of learning in our schools could certainly improve our kids' futures.

You may be looking at the title of this book and thinking, *Simplicity? A person couldn't live a simpler life than I am living these days.* But that is exactly the point of this book. Readers at all income levels should be able to extract something new from this book to apply to their lives immediately. There is always something we can change to boost our quality of life. We all need an occasional reminder of the importance of resetting our priorities, or at least fine-tuning them, which is exactly what America appears to currently be doing. We need to wake up! We have some real problems here. For at least the last fifteen years, we have made a number of mistakes, big blunders that helped feed this boom-and-bust economy in which we now live.

America once (recently!) had an economically vibrant middle class. Roads and bridges were well maintained, and our impressive and ever-growing infrastructure was the envy of the world. People were optimistic, and with good reason. The middle-class lifestyle was within reach of many Americans, including our immigrant population. Our work ethic and high expectations kept us striving toward a better future. People in America were always looking forward.

However, as difficult a time as this has been in America, we must always remember the gifts that we have been given in this beautiful land. I still believe that if given a choice to choose which country they could live in, most people would choose to live in the United States. For several years now I have worked with the International Student Exchange Program as a volunteer. It is my job to recruit families to host in their home a high school teen from another country. This has been a wonderful experience for me as well as for the kids from all over the world trying to make their dream come true by spending one school year in America. I am their contact while here in this country, so we meet in person on a quarterly basis. I'm in contact with them by phone and computer between visits to make sure they are getting along well in school and with their host family. I have found that each young person who comes here loves it. I have had the privilege of seeing our country through their eyes. Over the years I have hosted teens from Venezuela, Thailand, China, Germany, France, Spain, Brazil, Italy, and Tunisia. In fact, I still keep in contact with Roberto, in Brazil, and Kholoud, a Muslim teenager from Tunisia who hopes to come back to America to study at a U.S. medical school. Why am I mentioning this here? Because I wish to remind everyone that countries around the world still look toward America as a land where everyone has an opportunity to do well, which is a lot more than can be said about some other countries. So, whether during the good times or the bad, I'm happy I live in the United States.

We have historic unemployment in today's America with millions of people jobless and having no clue when or if they will find their next job. Quite honestly, it has felt anything but simple! Many Americans have become overwrought and tense about their financial stability, as our debt has gone up and the economy turned south. Clearly, some of America's irresponsible consumption habits caught up with us. And then it was shocking to see so many people losing their homes. This was beginning to look like a new America.

* * * * * * * * *

Chapter 2
A Tale of Two Nations: The Vanishing American Middle Class

* * * * * * * * *

Those who make peaceful revolution impossible will make violent revolution inevitable.

—John F. Kennedy

How did this happen? Well, we can start with the events of the seventies and eighties. At that time, our government deregulated and privatized many different businesses to the benefit of large corporations' bottom lines. At the same time, it was increasing the cost of public higher education and cutting public transportation. It shredded safety nets. It halved the top income tax rate, from the range of 70 to 90 percent that prevailed during the 1950s and 1960s, to 28 to 40 percent. It allowed many of the nation's rich to treat their income as capital gains subject to no taxes.

What Began as Cutbacks Grew Into Inequality

Next, corporations were allowed to slash jobs and wages, cut benefits, and shift risks to employees (from you-can-count-on-it pensions to do-it-yourself 401(k)s, and from good health coverage to soaring premiums and deductibles). The corporations busted unions (sounds familiar to what just transpired in Wisconsin!) and threatened employees who tried to organize. The biggest companies went global with no more loyalty or connection to the United States than a GPS device. And nothing was done to impede CEO salaries from skyrocketing to more than three hundred times that of the typical worker (from thirty times during the Great Prosperity of the 1950s and 1960s). These inequalities in our society should worry the average Americans, who are being left out in the cold. As the money rose to the top, so has political power. Politicians are more dependent than ever on big money for their campaigns. The bulk of today's political campaigns get funded through ever-increasing campaign donations from corporate executives and Wall Street, their ever-bigger platoons of lobbyists, and their hordes of PR flacks. Even foreign businesses participate in contributing to their favorite U.S. candidates. And now, in my opinion, we have had probably one of the worst Supreme Court verdicts issued in my memory. On January 10, 2010, the U.S. Supreme Court issued a ruling that struck down limits on corporate campaign spending. In effect, this treats a corporation, whether American or foreign, as if it is an individual voter. Of course, I do not know too many people who can donate millions to political campaigns and have the same deep pockets as an IBM or Proctor & Gamble. Do you?

Can an Oligarchy Possibly Happen in America?

You might be wondering whether this could really happen in a democracy. And if we don't begin to resist this oligarchy form of government—which is when most of the political power effectively rests within a small segment of society (typically the most powerful, whether by wealth, military strength, ruthlessness, or political influence), and the middle class and poor of a nation are left fewer and fewer choices—democracy will become the pile of ashes our kids and grandkids will play in.

New York Times writer Bob Herbert wrote in his column titled "Losing Our Way" on March 26, 2011, "This inequality, in which an enormous segment of the population struggles while the fortunate few ride the gravy train, is a world-class recipe for social unrest. Downward mobility is an ever-shortening fuse leading to profound consequences." As Herbert so vividly points out, if we don't get our act together and begin treating all Americans with the respect they deserve by lending support in difficult times and allowing all voices to be heard, then we will have failed as a democracy.

None of us can thrive in a nation divided between a small number of people receiving an ever-larger share of the nation's income and wealth, and everyone else receiving a declining share. This sort of lopsidedness would only diminish our economic growth and also tear at the social fabric of our society. The most fortunate among us who have reached the pinnacle of economic power and success depend on a stable economic and political system. That stability rests on the public's trust that the system operates in the interest of us all.

Divorce rates are always a reliable indicator of financial distress, as marriage counselors report that a high proportion of couples they see are experiencing significant financial problems. The areas suffering from the biggest wage loss in America also are reporting the largest increases in divorce rates, which is no surprise to divorce counselors.

The middle-class squeeze has also reduced voters' willingness to support even basic public services. Rich and poor alike endure crumbling roads, weak bridges, an unreliable rail system, and cargo containers that enter our ports without scrutiny. And many Americans live in the shadow of poorly maintained dams that could collapse at any moment.

But now for the good news! Yes, the rich can now buy bigger mansions and host more expensive parties, but this appears to have made them no happier. And in our winner-take-all economy, recent studies in the field of positive psychology show that thinking that people are happier the more successful they are is actually backward. Actually, it is happiness that fuels success, not the other way around. No one dares to argue that this rising inequality in America is fair or good. So why don't we all just try to stop ignoring what is happening here and agree that this is a bad thing for our country? That's simple enough, right? And that is what a Simplicity Revolution should be all about, simply addressing America's problems without emotions, just facts.

I found this next statement very prophetic and scary. In February 2003, Pulitzer Prize–winning writer Norman Mailer stated in his book, *Gaining an Empire, Losing Democracy?*

> *America is going to become a mega-banana republic where the army will have more and more importance in Americans' lives. It will be an ever greater and greater overlay on the American system. And before it is all over, democracy, noble and delicate as it is, may give way. My long experience with human nature suggests that it is possible that fascism, not democracy, is the natural state. Indeed, democracy is a special condition—a condition we will be called upon to defend in the coming years. That will be enormously difficult because the combination of the corporation, the military and the complete investiture of the flag with mass spectator sports has set up a pre-fascistic atmosphere in America already.*

This is scary stuff. What really concerns me about Mailer's warning is that it now appears to almost have been a prediction. I read into Mailer's warning that we should beware if the military budget in our nation overshadows all other expenses in this nation (like it is doing), when the wealth of our nation is held by a small percentage of the richest people in the country (which they now do), and finally, when it appears as if the big corporations are running our government (just take a look at the lobbying money spent by these big corporations and it tells us the truth).

Something here feels broken. And I certainly hope that more will be done to get this fixed before we continue to jeopardize our precious democracy. Just as we would defend our country against an invasion, an attack from another country, everybody should stand together to defend our democracy. This is a challenge we definitely need to face down, regardless of how difficult. Losing what we have built in this country is unacceptable. We must do a better job defending our precious democracy, as Mailer warned.

What America Means to the World

What remains most impressive about America is that we are the only country in the world that has so cleverly woven its society together from many. We've developed a societal and governmental structure that accommodates and protects the interests of all, so all residents have an equal stake in the game—that is, until recently. All you have to do to understand what I mean is look at our military. Not many Ivy League young men or women are heading off to fight wars.

Today America is still good at developing new technologies. We brought to the world the mass-produced automobiles, telephones, radio, electric lightbulbs, airplanes, movies, and television. As if that wasn't enough, Americans produced the Internet, Google, Yahoo, Skype, the iPhone, Twitter, and Facebook. A pretty amazing record, isn't it? So what could be next? What new genius is about to launch another world-changing invention? And chances are whenever that next jaw-dropping technology is launched on the world stage, it will once again come out of America. Why do I say this? Because I believe our American culture has always honored entrepreneurs and encouraged their development of new ways to think.

I worry about what will happen to our research funding if our government no longer is willing or able to invest in research and innovation. Can we really rely on rich Americans to pick up the tab? America's inventiveness could be severely damaged by what is currently being done in Congress. Some legislators are using the deficit to fire up their constituents. They are constantly framing budget issues around the deficit. The mind-set in Washington of late reminds me of that saying, "Be careful not to throw the baby out with the bathwater." If these individuals are thinking only of protecting their jobs ahead of the welfare of our nation, they really don't belong in Congress. For our country to cut back on research funding at this crucial time, with technology developing at such a fast pace, would be ludicrous. We must be prepared to keep ahead of the curve. Without question, our country is going to need the kinds of jobs that these new generations of technology and innovation may provide.

How much longer will it take before the poor and middle-class voters wake up and quit voting against their own self-interests? Our government cannot go on as a democracy by pretending greed does not take over. Maybe if billionaires and multimillionaires paid their fair share of taxes, I've heard it said that this national debt could get paid off in twenty years. Someone has to pay for all these wars, you know? The biggest excuse we hear time and time again is that the wealthy will use the money to create more jobs. But they sure have done a fine job of hiding all of those jobs they've been busily creating since the Bush tax cut initially became law leaving many Americans asking, "Where's the jobs?"

Chapter 3
Can't We Be A Big Happy Family?

* * * * * * * * *

You must look into other people as well as at them.
—Lord Chesterfield (1584–1656),
an English aristocrat

As challenging as it is, I believe the answer to the above question is "Yes!" Not only should we behave more as one big family, but looking forward that is what is needed for us to continue the growth of the American spirit, the great American dream. Yet, here we are today fighting political party versus political party. Haven't the recent negative attitudes people show toward our government gotten nauseating? Have you noticed how it is complicating the way Congress functions and even the way campaigns are run today (those commercials we must endure until we could scream)? It's all such a waste of money! I have often thought how ironic it is that just a decade ago everyone seemed so patriotic toward our country. Now all we hear is the spilling of ugly comments about our politicians. Often they are snarled at as if the word "politician" is dirty and poisonous. It really makes me wonder how anyone could still be willing to serve in Congress—or any political position, for that matter.

Because I have always been somewhat politically active in my community, a friend recently asked me if I was interested in running for some kind of elected office. You could have knocked me over with a feather! "Where did you get that idea?" I asked her. She replied, "Well, you just know so many people." After I stopped laughing, I told her, "First of all, I wouldn't even consider running for dog catcher! And second, I would never have the patience and energy!" And as sad as it is for me to say, there are some current senators and representatives now in Congress with whom I probably would find it very hard to work with, and vice versa.

There is so much at stake right now in our country. We need people to begin thinking once again like Abraham Lincoln, FDR, or John F. Kennedy. These people knew what our greatest strengths as a nation were. They encouraged people to think of this country as a place where everyone could coexist together, comfortably. I like to think of Lincoln's famous words spoken following the Civil War, which nearly tore us apart. He said, "With malice toward none, with charity for all." So let us try to rely on Lincoln's words once again and stop all of the silliness we see happening on our political front. Moving forward, let's hope all members of our American family will honor Lincoln's words and that these disruptive political party disputes will come to an end.

Here are just a few of the reasons we need to keep our government strong. We really need what our government does for us on a daily, monthly, and annual basis. Our government regulatory agencies are dedicated to overseeing the environmental, financial, insurance, food, and drug regulations. Believe me, we really would not want to face a future without these strong government regulatory agencies watching over businesses. These regulatory agencies act as our watchdog and, in fact, provide us with some assurances that all of us can live healthier and safer lives. Without them looking at some of these big corporations, I know I wouldn't feel too safe. How would I know that, when I take a Tylenol capsule for a headache, the chemicals put into that tablet are what the bottle says they are? I think it would be like feeding time in a shark tank without our federal regulators. Another example is the food we buy to feed ourselves and our families. If there wasn't someone looking over the shoulders of some of these huge corporate farms, how could you be sure that the chicken, beef, salmon we purchase hasn't been fed on a diet of chemicals in their food? As you can imagine, the list just goes on and on.

Here is how I imagine it. If we didn't have federal regulations looking after our interest, it could become like feeding time in a shark tank. If you've ever seen one, you know it's not pretty. It's just a feeding frenzy of those big guys killing off the little guys. They take as much food (money) as they can without concern for their (size advantage). We all need protection from those sharks, don't we?

Senator Al Franken identifies in an essay how voters today only want to hear simple answers when, in effect, there are no simple answers to some of the big problems facing America. Senator Franken wrote, "We may know the dangers in reaching for simple solutions subconsciously, but we tend to like it when we hear it." He continued, "There is no question that today's voters are drawn to politicians who seem to offer simple answers to complex problems. Election campaigns have become contests of reducing intricate complexities to an easy-to-swallow pill. Our allegiance to leaders—any leader—is available with one condition. People just want someone who is going to make it simple for them to understand." And many of us can be fooled by the simple promises made by some politicians, because we yearn for simplicity and just want someone to take care of the problems. Simplicity in this area of your life is not necessarily a good thing. You always have to listen between the lines!

Are America's Best Days Behind Us?

I used to laugh when my son's teenage friend Derrick would compare the sinking of our status as a world superpower to the final days of the Roman Empire. Now I can see where he was heading with this analogy!

A handful of American oligarchs are becoming megabillionaires, while it appears the rest of the country is going down the drain. The tax breaks to the rich were supposedly based on the concept that they were going to use the money to create jobs. We can now see they haven't created new jobs but have used the money to feather their own nests. The U.S. unemployment rate is currently the worst since the Great Depression. My friend Donald likes to say, "The trickle-down economy has never worked. It really is the effect of what we poor and middle-class people feel while those rich folks are pissing on us!" I fear that if we don't somehow address this societal disruption, eventually we could be facing real class warfare in this country. Leave it to my friend Donald to always paint such an eventful picture.

On May 8, 2011, economist Paul Krugman wrote in the *New York Times*, "The United States has mass long-term unemployment for the first time since the 1930s." He goes on to explain, "These days Americans get constant lectures about the need to reduce the budget deficit. That focus in itself represents distorted priorities, since our immediate concern should be job creation." On this point, Mr. Krugman and I are on the same page. By restricting ourselves to talking about the federal deficit, we should all be asking those legislators who cling to this idea what's happened to that budget surplus the federal government had in 2000.

The first thing that probably comes to mind are the wars in Iraq and Afghanistan, which added approximately $1.1 trillion, but we must never forget that those Bush tax cuts added roughly $2 trillion to the national debt over the last decade. So there you have it! The largest U.S. deficit ever, in fact, is not directly linked to excessive out-of-control spending by Washington legislators. No, clearly it has happened due to careless, unwise decision making by the policy elite.

Many families today feel like they are barely holding on. They are pinched every month from every direction just to make ends meet. In the October 2010 *New York Times*, David Brooks wrote, "The nation's fear of decline and its current sour mood is not just caused by high unemployment. It emerges from the fear that America's best days are behind it." I think Mr. Brooks is on to something here. Perhaps our politicians will come to the realization that for years now the link between effort and reward has felt broken to many working Americans. Can anyone explain to me why the jobs of some of these investment bankers who pull in those million-dollar bonuses are compensated so much more than, say, a third grade teacher? Or, a policeman, a fireman, a scientist, a professor? I doubt it.

Once upon a time, we assumed growth would be endless. Then, America's optimism came to a standstill. Optimism had been a mainstay in America since the post–World War II days. Few of us expected this sort of economic slowdown would be more than a pause. And, when it hit, it felt like a ton of bricks had fallen on us. It is even hard for many of us to call this simply a recession, given the rising number of ghost towns, bankrupt businesses, defaults on homes, and falling prices of our economic mainstay—home buying—in America. So what are we going to do about it? Can we change what has happened? No. Can we start to look at it differently and start building for the future? Yes.

A Simplicity Revolution: Can It Help Us Regain Our Mojo?

I hope that, by reading this book and being attentive to its message, you can begin to see that what we really need in life cannot be purchased with credit cards or taken away by the greedy few who have pushed us into crisis of late. In fact, in some cases perhaps our own personal crises could have been minimized had we lived more simply before it happened. Well, at least now you can learn how to avert a debt crisis in the future. Maybe not entirely, but if you just turn your head and heart in a different, simpler direction, sometimes you can avoid the pain of owing too much on those credit cards. If we truly seek to make permanent changes, this current economy will force us to stare down our own personal issues. It is my hope, ultimately, to open minds to appreciate that there are so many things we can still do for ourselves. To those of you who think you need to purchase everything and have everything done for you, think again. I swear there are some people who would hire someone to breathe for them if they could. Yet, to get on the path of simplicity, we need to stop acting so helpless. Here's an example. Have you ever thought about this irony? Many Americans pay someone to do all of their yard work. I know it requires lots of lifting, bending, and moving around. In other words, it is an excellent workout. Nevertheless, they prefer to pay their monthly membership fees to a local health club where they can do what? Work out! Now that is somewhat humorous, isn't it? I know, going to the club is more fun and offers many benefits that cleaning up the yard does not. But having that moment of personal accomplishment when someone walking by your house compliments you on how nice your house and garden look, will be the added bonus to those pounds you were able to work off outside on a beautiful day. From 2008 until December 2010, our economy became too inflated, and perhaps we needed to be reminded that it could also be deflated. Perhaps your life needs a little more breathing room, and now is the time to begin taking a simpler view of what you need in life to make you happy. And, if you are a parent of young children, please try to teach them to be more self-sufficient than the last few generations before them. Sociologists report that the last few generations are seeing many kids who feel they are entitled to everything. I am convinced that the more America can rid itself of this feeling of entitlement in our population, the sooner we will be back on track to being the successful nation we have always been. It is through a Simplicity Revolution that I believe we will resurrect our American inventiveness and creativity, which is where many of our jobs of the future will come from.

Chapter 4
My Moment of Life
Clarity: A Simple Gift

Joy is not in things; it is in us!
—Benjamin Franklin

So why are more and more Americans embracing elements of old-fashioned traditions, such as canning their own jam, growing greens in container gardens on apartment balconies, and fencing off a portion of their suburban lots for beehives? I believe it is a way for people to connect with the past while also attempting to simplify their present and future. In other words, people are back to preserving some of the cultural heritage from our parents. Perhaps this is a way to quietly defy the frenzy of modern-day life. It certainly contrasts how most of us tend to live our contemporary lifestyles, doesn't it?

Recently, I visited a local Amish general store in Bulls Gap, Tennessee, and it provided me with a marvelous look into our heritage. I found so many homemade products there that I never thought people could actually make on their own. That is an example of how far removed we, as a society, have become. People who live in the city don't ever think that perhaps they could make some of these things themselves. Baking breads and cakes is still something we all feel capable of, but there were all kinds of jams, soaps, nonprocessed grains, etc., that I found at this Amish store. I actually remember getting a thrill out of purchasing the dish soap and laundry detergent because it wasn't from a Procter & Gamble sort of company. The Amish store itself was celebrating simplicity—and doing it in a splendid way.

I think many people are trying to build a safer and saner future, a lifestyle that is not drowning in debt and "stuff." On the Internet, there are all kinds of homesteader groups that connect on Meetup.com to swap tips and plan workshops on everything from beer making to composting to gardening, proving there are many people in search of living more simply.

What compels most people to adopt a Simplicity Revolution is having what I call a moment of "life clarity." I will now share with you my story that led to having such a moment. If you are like me, it may require something profound happening in your life to get you wanting and needing a simpler and saner life. I'd begun to realize that I needed to let go of looking for happiness from "stuff" and to search for a deeper meaning for my life. The antiquing I'd always loved became more of a burden than a joy—in other words, a complicated commitment more than just a fun hobby. It just wasn't working for me anymore. A feeling of growing dissatisfaction was developing, and that was when I noticed I needed to let go of looking for happiness in "stuff" and start searching deeper for something with real, lasting meaning in my life. For some people, this can be a religious moment, but I don't want to paint it that way. It can be whatever you think it is. You can talk to a hundred different baby boomers, bootstrappers, Generation Xers, whatever; you'll likely get a hundred different answers for what motivates someone to do something. I'd already had my first real eye-opening moment before trying my hand at antiques. That moment came when I was forty-four years of age. Like most heart attacks, mine was totally unexpected, and I had to have an emergency angioplasty surgery at 2:30 a.m. because I had a dissected artery that luckily they were able to repair by deploying three stents into the artery. Because I did not have any of the usual risk factors for this sort of heart event, it was especially shocking. I told my friend Bob Thompson the next day, "Who would have thought I was at risk for this?" He replied, "Sue, we are all at risk from the moment we are born!" This is something I have never forgotten, and it has changed my approach to life. My dear son, Alex, was only nine years old at the time. I can only imagine how upsetting that whole event was for him.

I was still in the cardiac intensive care unit one evening later that week. It was a Saturday night, following a busy day of visits from family and friends. I was sitting in this silent room, experiencing an incredible sense of happiness, serenity, love, and satisfaction. In this moment of total peace, I was overcome with a sense of clarity. I thought, *Life is so fragile!* What was the meaning of my life? In less than a second, it came to me. We all have to define it for ourselves, but the meaning of *my* life is relationships. The "stuff" I'd been gathering along the way was totally immaterial to my being, my happiness. Real pleasure for me comes from spending time with family and friends, creating new friends, and having a good laugh. These are truly the kinds of things that I cherish and that fulfill me.

A few years later I ran into a scheduling conflict. I had planned a trip out of town because I'd forgotten a friend's invitation to her backyard cookout. I started realizing I'd rather sit in my friend's backyard than fly out of town for a weekend trip, so that is what I did, and it felt good. It felt absolutely right. This was when I also finally found the meaning of the saying, "The best things in life are free." And I'm not talking about the free meal at my friend's house, but the freedom of choosing the simpler, less chaotic way.

I think I have always been very adept at recognizing trends when they are brewing, and this definitely has been one of those times. Around 2007, I began observing people all around me who wanted to begin living clean lifestyles, downsize, and reduce their consumption. Now, you could say this is coming about entirely because of the Great Recession, because of our uncertain economy. Or maybe the aging baby boomers are just doing what comes naturally as they age (i.e., simplifying and downsizing). But I believe that people were coming to realize that their lives of abundance didn't necessarily fulfill them. When the economic chill hit the proverbial fan, we couldn't help but be angry with the greedy money lenders and investment deal makers. We needed to pull away from them. We were creating a new era in America, one that reflected back to our old values and tried to bring them to the forefront once again. Should the economy start to turn around considerably, does anyone honestly think we will see everything going back to exactly as it was, say, in January 2008? As a homeowner, even though I would love to see our home values climb back up to where they were, I doubt they will. This depends on who you believe, but I am hearing projections as far out as 2014 before we will see the housing market begin to recover. Like you, I also am hoping to see our economy recover sooner than that, but accepting that expression, "It is what it is," really can be quite calming.

Everywhere you look today you can see a craving for more simplicity. The anger and frustration in our culture was getting far too intense. Whereas before when people got upset they might have a few ugly words to say, now people get crazier, and louder, and their fuses are much shorter. Recognizing this, we began asking ourselves if maybe life was getting just a little too intense. We began wondering how we could lessen this intensity, and the answer was that we couldn't do anything about the way others were living, but we certainly could control the way we were living, which has also added to the need for a Simplicity Revolution. It was time for America to do a little introspection, a self-checkup. I like to think of it as a tune-up for our cars, so this is the time for America's tune-up!

The way we view the planet, our natural resources, our country, and ultimately each other has changed at great speed. Quaker Elder Joseph Brackett Jr. could never have imagined where society was headed when he wrote the song "Simple Gifts" in 1848. These are the lyrics to his still-poignant one-verse song, which still hold true today:

'Tis the gift to be simple, 'tis the gift to be free,
'Tis the gift to come down where we ought to be,
And when we find ourselves in the place just right,
It will be in the valley of love and delight.
When true simplicity is gained,
To bow and to bend we shan't be ashamed,
To turn, turn will be our delight,
Till by turning, turning we come round right.

In 1848, this song was greatly valued in the Quaker community. And to this day, the song is beloved, not just among Quakers but among the wider American religious communities and even folk music lovers. I am not suggesting that everyone living in today's decade take a time machine backward to the 1800s. I do think, however, that we could all benefit by being more attentive toward people around us, such as smiling at the grocery clerk who is checking you out or taking a moment to speak with your house painter as he is cleaning up. Spend a few minutes getting to know your neighbors. Remember to take a moment every day to either enjoy yourself or help to bring enjoyment to another.

Psychologist Robert Wicks, a psychology professor at Loyola University, Maryland, notes that in the "up economy, people were successful, but in many cases, they were missing their lives." He added, "They weren't spending time really enjoying life and weren't spending time with family and friends. The simplicity that's possible during these difficult economic times would not come to the fore if this crisis had not occurred."

Living a simpler life requires approaching your daily life in a more mindful way. Mindfulness is being present for what is happening in your life and is sometimes associated with the Buddhist meditation way of life. I think that the gift of mindfulness is the greatest gift you will ever give yourself, and it is perhaps why over the ages it has been written about by some of the world's great thinkers. In fact, I like to think that if our greatest philosophers (i.e., Plato, Socrates, Aristotle) were still alive, they would be in favor of moving forward with a Simplicity Revolution. Ultimately, simplicity is about knowing who you are. The key is having a firm value system by which you share your life with other people. It is also about learning how to live happily outside of the material world, which with all the marketing around us at times can feel like quite a challenge.

Families today are frightened. At times we feel like we are being forced to walk a tightrope over the molten lava that was once firm ground. As I said before, where once we assumed endless upward economic growth would continue, we now found that it didn't. Had endless upward growth ever been possible? Probably not! Our overindulgences as a society either went unnoticed or were willfully swept under the rug. I suppose things were so good. so why invite negativity? But since the 1970s, the vast majority of working Americans gradually came to see that their personal income had grown stagnant. The results were inevitably a growing loss of income on the middle class and poor. These diminishing incomes left some people to feel powerless and impotent. Now, many Americans are coming to the realization that the long-held assumption that their children's generation will have it better than our current generation is just not holding up any longer, and it saddens us.

Chapter 5
Four Guideposts to a Simpler Life

* * * * * * * * *

Personal transformation can and does have global effects. As we go, so goes the world, for the world is us. The revolution that will save the world is ultimately a personal one.
—Marianne Williamson

If you are wondering how to create a path to simpler living, I suggest using these four guideposts: First, protect our environment. This means safeguard our planet, all creatures big and small, and all plant life. Second, always be financially responsible. Third, use thoughtful consumption. And fourth, stay involved in your community.

I believe when you attend to these four areas of your life, you will be better able to live a full, happy, and simple lifestyle that is doable and measurable and that everyone is capable of achieving. Now let's take a look at each one of these elements separately.

Protect our environment.

If ever there was a need in America for more environmental awareness, it is now. As Elizabeth Seton (1774–1821)—who on September 14, 1975, was canonized, making her the first native-born U.S. citizen to become a saint—said, "Americans must learn to live simply so that others may simply live their lives." I love this quote, because with so very few words, it succinctly captures the message I hope my book conveys.

I hope that, as part of your attempt to simplify your life, you embrace living a greener life and encourage those around you to do so, as well. Rather than going over all of the ways to go green, I suggest that you Google "green living." A wide assortment of ideas will pop up that you can begin to incorporate into your daily life. I would hope all of us could agree that, out of respect for this magnificent planet we have been given, we want to be sure to leave only a green footprint behind. I recognize that there are still some people who do not believe that climate change is really happening in a destructive way. Based on all of my investigative findings concerning this issue, I have seen how real scientists around the world are viewing this threat. And they are treating this as a very real threat—if not directly to me or my family, to various animal species and plant and sea life. And once we lose a species, it stays gone.

The facts are devastatingly clear. Here are just some of the problems climate change has begun to facilitate around the globe. We saw the hottest year yet in 2010. From the flooding in Pakistan, to the increased volcanic eruptions in Indonesia, to droughts in Russia, and to landslides in China, the effects of this year's extreme weather are catastrophic and undeniable. The recent pattern of extreme weather events is consistent with what scientists have projected to result from climate change: temperature shifts, severe rainfall, more snow in some parts of the world, and major droughts in others. More than 1,500 people have died in Pakistan's northwest, and 4 million people were stranded after the deadliest floods in eighty years struck in July 2010. Five percent of the nation's rice crop has been damaged, the Rice Exporters Association reported, and at least 1.8 million people urgently need food, according to the United Nations World Food Program.

In North Korea, rains triggered landslides that blocked railways, destroyed homes, and buried crops, piling on hardship for a country that already needs aid to feed its 24 million people. Floods in China have killed at least 1,072 people this year, affecting 9.7 million hectares of farmland, according to the government.

China had its worst floods in more than a decade, cutting rice and pork production, boosting prices, and hampering government efforts to keep inflation under 3 percent. Rice output may fall 5 percent to 7 percent, according to Shanghai JC Intelligence Co.

"While on the opposite side of the world, dry weather is also affecting the winter wheat crop production in Western Australia," said David Streit, senior lead forecaster with Commodity Weather Group in Bethesda, Maryland. "The markets are starting to focus on this, as wheat production is so tight right now," Streit said. As the evidence mounts, leaders like Russian President

Dmitry Medvedev are speaking out about climate change. President Medvedev spoke out at a United Nations Security Council meeting: "What is happening now in our central regions is evidence of this global climate change, because we have never in our history faced such weather conditions in the past. This means that we will need to change the way we work from the methods that we used in the past." Adding to the trouble in Russia are forest and peat-bog fires east of Moscow that have shrouded the city in smoke and delayed as many as 140 flights at the capital's airport. Carbon monoxide in Moscow's air rose to as high as 4.8 times the admissible maximum level before tapering off slightly toward evening, the city's environmental protection department said on its website. The Health Ministry was advising Russians to stay indoors, limit physical activity, and wear masks when venturing outside. Emergency crews were battling 558 fires covering 179,596 hectares (693 square miles) across Russia, the Emergency Situations Ministry said. In 2010, fires had scorched 729,761 hectares, an area about three times the size of Luxembourg, according to the ministry, and worst of all the fires killed at least fifty-two people, the Health Ministry.

As of May 1, 2011, there have been 1,196 tornadoes reported in the United States (of which at least 575 were confirmed during the first five months of the year). We have had 406 deaths, due in large part to several extremely large tornado outbreaks in the middle and end of April, making this year the deadliest from tornadoes since 1953. As with any major weather disaster these days— from floods and hurricanes to wildfires and the recent tornado outbreak in the South—people ask questions about its relation to global climate change. Since 2007, two separate studies reported that global warming could bring a dramatic increase in the frequency of weather conditions that feed severe thunderstorms and tornadoes by the end of the twenty-first century. The fuel for the more intense storms would be the predicted warming of the Earth caused by the burning of fossil fuels that release greenhouse gases, according to a report by study lead author Jeff Trapp of Purdue University.

As you can see around the world, the changing climate is already wreaking havoc in some very weird ways. According to LiveScience.com, which chronicles daily scientific advances, we need to prepare ourselves for more such strange effects as those savage wildfires, disappearing lakes, and the threat of long-gone diseases reemerging.

Remember, the window for effective action is closing fast, and responding to the climate crisis will take commitment and ingenuity. The actions we take in the next several years will determine the kind of world future generations will inherit. I sincerely believe that it will only be through thoughtful and committed movements, such as a Simplicity Revolution, that we can gain the attention of the 300 million people in our U.S. community and encourage them to slow down and listen to our planet and hopefully begin spreading the word to other global communities around the world.

Always pay close attention to legislation, which affects our environment. Sign on as an objector to the passage of legislation when you see a bill being introduced in

Congress that would be negative for the environment. The big corporations have shown they really don't care what condition they leave our land and seas in, so it is up to all of us to let the business world know that we care about our environment and will be protecting it with everything we've got. And, never accept those naysayers who say things like "You can never beat city hall." We definitely can beat back legislation that we feel is not to our society's benefit.

The strength of these large corporations, the moneyed in this country, may seem unbeatable, but that is not true. When people unite on issues because of their beliefs, they can have an incredible effect on the outcome. Here is a recent example. On March 14 and 15, 2011, a friend and I drove to Madison, Wisconsin, to march in protest against Republican Governor Walker's controversial plan that stripped teachers, nurses, highway workers, and other public employees of most of their collective bargaining rights. Over 100,000 people turned out in protest, and signatures were gathered to move forward to recall not only the governor, but many legislators who have supported this outright attack on organized labor in our country. As we, the objectors, were walking around the state capital, we were chanting as we marched: "Tell me what democracy looks like. This is what democracy looks like!" The mood of the crowd was that of long-lost friends reuniting. Every person was so respectful of everyone else. It was a weekend that will stay in my memory a very long time. I felt very happy that I had taken the time to participate in objecting to the injustice that was transpiring. Believing that you can make a difference, as some of you have experienced, is truly a lifting moment for a person's soul.

Always be financially responsible.

Cultural changes in America are constant. Sometimes it's cyclical and sometimes not. Despite our love for overindulging ourselves, there were signs that major changes to our lifestyles were in the air. And for those who were already feeling economically pinched, this economic slowdown has made life even tougher for them. We now are seeing more and more food banks running out of food because it is not just the poor showing up, but it is also many middle-class Americans who never before had to rely on going to a food bank for food in order to eat and stay alive.

Certain weaknesses in our lifestyle went either unnoticed or ignored for too long until the balloon popped. Our lives, which had grown bloated, spoiled, and accustomed to certain comfort levels, left us early on in this economic downturn feeling like we were being deprived. To that, I would like to say, "Try telling that to someone living in a Third World country who doesn't know where his next meal will be coming from."

Americans can cope with these changes in lifestyle, but in many cases it will force us to contend with rearranging our plans, hopes, and dreams for our future. In some cases, a person went from having a doable retirement to no retirement whatsoever, or at least not the sort of retirement many of our parents may have been able to have. Yes, life was changing in America, and we needed to face up to the fact that the images many of us had carried in our heads was only that, an image. And as times have changed, so must those visions. We need to look at these changes as a new opportunity, even though the answer is not yet clear what these new opportunities will look like.

Use thoughtful consumption.

It is important to create a thoughtful consumer out of everyone, which will be really tough on some people.

Our unending hunger for "stuff" resulted in chaos, which is why perhaps we need to begin living easier, lighter, humbler lives once again. We should recognize how many addictions we have, and it's not just to drugs and fossil fuels! Yes, America, it is time to rush off of this unsustainable path. Let's abandon our "stuff" addiction.

Toward the end of our last decade, people began feeling tired of being squeezed from purchasing more "stuff" than they needed. What made this even more of a problem for so many Americans was that they had begun living beyond their means, which was made possible by the ever-growing use credit.

Here is what now needs to happen. In fact, I believe it has already begun. Beginning with this new decade, after the crash, a simpler life shall be emerging. It will be slower, more thoughtful, and will contain far fewer things. The benefits of living a simpler life will be improved health, more time, and living with the knowledge that your life is in your own hands. It can mean a degree of freedom from the impact of Wall Street's greed. Living a simpler life can also include the knowledge that you are doing something proactive to improve the lives of others by reducing your impact on the environment. For example, buy organic, fair-trade, or locally grown products that improve others' lives.

Stay involved in your community.

Each of us holds more power than we believe we have, and working together as a group, we can unite on a cause of action and move mountains. Working as a united force teaches us the meaning of living a more thoughtful life by showing a higher regard for life, our planet, and ourselves. For example, if each person simplifies his life, could we perhaps bring some sanity back to our society? Who isn't sick and tired of seeing such crazy, uncivil antics being publicly displayed? This applies to not only our youth, but also adults. Getting our nation off of the self-destructive course it has been on, will require us to work together to once again begin re-emphasizing our values system in this country to young and old.

So many people living in America today are accustomed to getting what they want when they want it, whether or not they have the money to pay for it. I don't think that the worship of "stuff" has ever been greater. Honestly, I am not against needed consumerism by any means. I think we just got too excited about all of those low-cost imported items we could buy at Walmart, and soon we were filling our homes with much more than we needed. And we were driven to keep buying more from those stores that always featured lower prices. As I said, I'm not against shopping; after all, that is what drives our economy. Let's face it, shopping can be fun, but not when the debt starts piling up and the finance charges start complicating your life. Heck, that's one kind of fun that nobody needs!

I fought with myself to not use the term "stuff" in this book because I thought it was a rather silly, lazy word. But I kept coming back to it. "Possessions" sounds too academic. "Stuff" only began to make sense when I recognized our habits in America have become juvenile. The word "stuff" is simply correct, and therein was the irony of our times. It is an innocuous word describing a large, ridiculous problem. Literally, America's "stuff" was squeezing, burdening, and encumbering our lives to a breaking point. Remember, the "stuff" we purchase requires someone to work to pay for the "stuff."

Chapter 6
Look Around: A Simplicity Revolution Has Begun

We must be willing to let go of the life we had planned, so as to accept the life that is waiting for us.

—Joseph Campbell

Following are twelve signs that a Simplicity Revolution has already begun. I am quite sure everyone will be able to add many more ways that they can identify such signs in their everyday lives.

Sign 1

In an effort to simplify our way of eating, America's "organic" craze is no longer for health-food nuts only. Organic products are now marketed in major supermarkets across the country, and the industry is enjoying double-digit annual growth. While some consumers think of organic food as boxed cereals or turkey bacon, new categories are now seen across the country. The category has become so much more, including items like wine and even caviar. Thanks to mass marketing and health-conscious consumers who favor foods without synthetic herbicides, pesticides, and hormones, organics have arrived! People want to eat healthily, natural, simple foods, like generations before us once did.

And here is more evidence that Americans are eating cleaner and simpler foods. The organic food sales at a retail level totaled $10.4 billion in 2009, according to Katherine DiMatteo, executive director of the Organic Trade Association. Perhaps that's why the major food corporations that never before concentrated on offering consumers organic products are now busy trying to buy companies with organic products.

As our awareness continues to grow about the food we eat, you would have to be living on a different planet to not know that people are disgusted with and questioning how their food is produced. More and more people seek ways to eliminate chemicals and other contaminants in our food chain. In America, most farmers went from being a one-barn family farm to those mega-corporate farms that can produce a meat supply of pigs, hens, and cows, unlike any other country in the world. But with this approach to raising our animals in such confined, restricted areas, the need to treat them with antibiotics and other additives grew greater. Therefore, organically raised meat is also higher in demand and in price.

Sign 2

A decade ago, this would have seemed improbable, but today, cities across the country, including New York

City, are allowing homeowners to keep chickens in their yards for those free-range eggs, giving city dwellers the ability to avoid industrially produced eggs. Last time I checked, there appeared to be over one hundred cities across America that allowed backyard chickens. Now doesn't that sound like an incredible way to eat some very edible eggs at their freshest?

Sign 3

The brown-bag lunch is now back in vogue. Remember when people would attempt to hide those sack lunches from coworkers? No way did you want to give the impression that you could not afford to eat lunch out. Well, that certainly is no longer the case. People are brown-bagging it for lunch more than ever to save money, and they no longer hide those bags from coworkers. These brown baggers can be seen everywhere, with the exception of Wall Street. After all, some pretensions are too valuable to give up!

Sign 4

Instead of wanting McMansion-type residential building designs, the U.S. Census Bureau recently reported that the median new home size fell to 2,135 feet. People no longer are looking for spaces devoted to single purposes. The days of wanting one's own billiard room appear to be over. People now are thinking more about how to save money on utilities and taxes. Those single-family homes recently built from lot line to lot line appear to be a thing of the past.

Sign 5

Take a look around you and you'll see people carrying reusable shopping sacks at the farmer's markets or into grocery stores. We're beginning to look more European every day. We have become environmentally conscious and are trying to wean ourselves off the constant use of those plastic bags, which are bad for the environment. Anyone who doesn't understand why I say that has never had to look at the same plastic bag wrapped around the top of a tree for a full year. Poor tree!

Sign 6

People are more inclined to jump on a bicycle or walk than drive their car whenever possible. Additionally, more people are purchasing hybrid vehicles even though this type of vehicle costs more to purchase. People are beginning to show respect for the environment more than the almighty dollar.

Sign 7

Many people are now starting their own organic produce gardens in their backyards, regardless of how small their yard space. Although you could say this has always taken place, statistics show that more and more home gardeners are harvesting their own produce. The pride of caring for your own freedom garden has become contagious, and it is happening from coast to coast.

Sign 8

We now like to catch rain in our rain barrels to water

our organic gardens. If you don't have one, I highly recommend you purchase one. If you have a water bill where you live, this is one bill you can successfully reduce by using your own water that you collected in your rain barrel for watering your gardens and lawns.

Sign 9

Numerous people are using compact fluorescent lightbulbs, or CFLs, to save on energy. If you are not using them yet in your home, you probably don't want to admit this to friends or family. They may try shaming you over it! It was only a few years ago when I saw my first one. I thought, *God, that is ugly!* Little would I have guessed that they would go mainstream so quickly. They no longer look ugly to me; in fact, I like how they look, and they do save money on that electric bill!

Sign 10

Cremation is a growing trend in the United States. By 2010, it was included in 40 percent of all funerals, according to the Cremation Association of North America. Alternative methods of burial are being looked at, including eco-friendly or "green" burials, for burials that would have the least impact on the earth and its surroundings. The other reason more people are opting for cremation is that it is less expensive and considered to be much simpler. The rise of cremation acceptance is due to more environmental consideration, weaker ties to tradition, less regional loyalty, and the elimination of religious restrictions.

Sign 11

People are talking more than ever before about downsizing their lives in order to simplify their lifestyles. People realize that with all of that "stuff," there is a price. People are openly talking about simplifying their lives, so they are able to spend time enjoying their family and friends. It is as simple as that!

Sign 12

Many major grocery stores have developed their own "economy" products that people are choosing to buy over well-known brands, which can cost double. The days of spending three or four dollars on a bag of chips are over. Spending money wisely is back in vogue.

* * * * * * * * *

Chapter 7
Our American Family Values

* * * * * * * * *

Nothing is worth more than this day.
—Johann Wolfgang von Goethe

The term "family values" has been tossed around ad nauseam, so it got me to wondering about what Americans think our "family values" really are. People throughout time have always held some of the same ambitions and inhibitions as those of us living in the present. I came upon the research of Guy Reel, assistant professor of mass communication at Winthrop University in Charlotte, South Carolina. According to a paper he had on the Common Dreams website, "our sense of values throughout our country's history has remained the same for over the last one hundred years. America is a balancing act. Sometimes we slip off the wire, because it's always going to be a work in progress." That is how I am looking at Wall Street's recent painful lapse of integrity. Bernie Madoff and a few others slipped off the wire.

Here are the most highly rated American family values currently, as well as for the last one hundred years (and, yes, they are the same): family life, friendship, health, independence, enjoyment, creativity, and integrity.

As Professor Reel said, I have felt that over the past twenty years America has slipped off the wire, fallen off its foundation, or at the least it feels as if our foundation has cracked. Americans have gotten caught up with this "supersize everything" notion. More will not necessarily make something better, yet that became the trend, and before long some of us started to forget our core values. These are the same values that had served us well for over two hundred years, allowing our nation to sparkle.

The biggest detriment to our culture is our loss of a sense of community. Belonging to a community—where everyone knows everyone, not only on their block or in their building, but for blocks around—this once was a way that people felt they had someone to depend on for help, should they need a helping hand. It built a deep sense of security to one's neighborhood and family life. But in today's busy world, many neighborhoods can almost look empty during the daytime and evening. With two people working in a household, often getting neighbors to meet, much less know, each other becomes impossible. Once upon a time kids played outside, running up and down neighborhood streets, and in the summertime sometimes all day long. Now many kids like to play computer games inside, so they hardly get to know the other kids on the block.

I remember a time when people were welcomed into their new neighborhood by a local homeowner's group. These groups would quickly get you up to date on any new developments locally, and it was a fine way for people to feel connected to their new community. I'm sure many of these types of groups still exist across America; however, I know in my area the new homeowners moving in do not seem as community-oriented as people were just fifteen years ago. If you were to ask them why, their reply would probably be that they are too busy working and raising their families. But looking back, it appears that every earlier generation found time to devote to improving their communities while working and raising their families.

Recently, I had to go visit my doctor, who moved from downtown Chicago to a new location in Lake Forest, Illinois, which is just about twenty-five miles north of where I live in Evanston. This trip is like going from night to day. You wouldn't believe how well people live on Chicago's North Shore. If you have ever driven through some of the poorer areas on the South Side of Chicago, you can clearly see some of the failures of our American system of government. I couldn't help but notice that in the midst of this community's grandeur and wealth, it seemed empty of people outside going about their business on this fine sunny day. With so many big homes and properties, shouldn't there have been more people present besides lawn-care service people? In the suburb where I live, being next to Chicago, it really is very city like. There are always lots of people out walking to where they need to go, hurrying off to meet a friend, walking their dogs, or running to get to a meeting. It radiates energy and connectedness, which was something I wasn't quite feeling in this new area.

Each home I drove by was bigger and more beautiful than the next. Yet, it kept bothering me. Where were all the people? Where was everybody? As I was parking at the hospital where my appointment was, a person couldn't help but notice that every car was an expensive late-model BMW, Jaguar, or Mercedes Benz. It quickly became apparent that I was in the midst of that top 1 percent of our population. It made me want to begin interviewing some of the locals. My first question would be about how fair did they believe it was for them to continue receiving tax breaks while our nation was in such need of more tax revenue? The tax break that they had been receiving now for more than three years was suppose to lead to creating jobs, yet millions of jobs have been lost, not gained. How could they feel it was fair and that they should continue to receive their tax break and continue living their very comfy lives while many people in this country are struggling so greatly? Were they happy knowing that Congress cut federal programs for the poor, the sick, and the college graduates who have no easy way to pay back their college loans, while they were going to continue to benefit from their significant tax break? Something felt horribly wrong here.

The hospital lobby was very refined. The receptionist and her counter looked as if a person was checking into the Plaza Hotel in New York City. The furniture is hard to describe. Some people probably find it very attractive, but it made me want to laugh. I couldn't quite tell what kind of look they were going after. It looked like "colonial modern," if there is such a thing. Clearly, there was only one main intent here, and it was to let you know that they knew their clientele well, and as long as they could make the lobby look conservatively moneyed, they would have achieved their goal.

I had to wonder how my doctor was feeling in this new location, because he didn't strike me as having anything in common with what I was seeing. Upon meeting, we said the usual niceties to each other. Knowing he lives near me, I said, "Your commute must be much quicker now." He replied, "Yes, that's why I did this, so I could be home with my young kids more." Then he told me that many of his city patients, who were continuing to see him, had mentioned to him how different the offices were from his downtown Chicago office. I felt relieved that he'd brought this up first, because I just knew this didn't reflect him at all. He proceeded to tell me that he really is a "city kind of guy." I replied, "Well, I know I'm a city kind of gal." Next, we both had a good laugh at the expense of that conservatively moneyed look, which was stamped throughout. I suppose it just wasn't our kind of thing.

Can You Remember When Sundays Meant Family Day?

Remember when Sundays meant something very special to American families? Only now do I understand why these days were so special, even though every Sunday we did the same exact thing. Here was a typical family Sunday in my household. My parents and I would visit our grandparents. Grandma would guide us out to the yard to look over her garden. She would slowly walk around the whole garden as I listened carefully to her comments on each flowering plant. I remember her pointing out those bushes that disappointed her and, boy, did she ever covet those rose bushes every year!

Next, we would all wander to her kitchen, and she would begin baking a treat for us. Believe me, this baking did not come out of a box. During this time, my father and grandpa would be in the garage tooling around with the hopes they could keep my dad's Chevy Impala running for another month.

The family's entertainment on those visits consisted of conversation and listening to some records that Grandpa would play on his high-fidelity (hi-fi) music system. Eventually, Grandma would call everyone back to the kitchen for a piece of her freshly baked cherry pie with one small scoop of vanilla ice cream. The end of this weekly ritual came with all of us seated around the black-and-white RCA television in the living room (they didn't have family rooms in those days). We all eagerly proceeded to watch everyone's favorite hour of television, the *Ed Sullivan Show*!

All in all, a rather clean day of memorable living that I can still recall in such loving detail. Why am I calling this "clean living"? Because family days like this are so innocent, untainted, and simple. Just like our current modern family scenarios, right? Well, probably not! In today's lifestyle, Grandma and Grandpa are likely living hundreds of miles away, and the only time the whole extended family gets together is for a big holiday. If you have children, Sundays are probably filled with lots of kids' events, like soccer games, that can eat up a good portion of the day. What family doesn't have to take a son or daughter to an event on the weekends? Needless to say, kids today have busier schedules than they ever did before. At least they have more birthday parties to go to. With all of the extracurricular activities, spending a whole Sunday together relaxing and having fun simply doesn't happen. Or, if it does happen, it is usually for some special occasion, like a graduation or religious event.

As we have strayed away from living simply, we have developed this ongoing march toward an unsustainable, overly complex lifestyle. The pursuit of the almighty dollar appears to have become the basis of U.S. civilization, and ironically, now our civility erodes. I will explain what economists mean when they call today's economy "our new normal." In other words, gone are the days of "spend, baby, spend." At least for the time being, people are not as likely to throw caution to the wind. We are living in a time of historic unemployment, with millions of people jobless and having no clue whatsoever as to where, or even if, they will find their next job. For these people, survival alone requires absolute simplicity.

Because the younger generation has seen how their parents and friends were treated by their long-term employers, sociologists and psychologists are noting that many people are no longer willing to sacrifice family time for their corporate employers. They watched as their family members and friends were unceremoniously tossed on the unemployment scrap heap through downsizing and outsourcing. The "take care of your employer and it will take care of you" work ethic our parents taught us became a lie.

Later in the book, I will show you what some of our ancient great philosophers wrote about the topic of simplicity. I have found these works exceptionally beneficial. They have illuminated the topic, and I now believe simplicity is indeed a human need and is vital to our connection to the magnificent bodies we are given as well as the glorious planet we have been given. If you feel like you are ready for more simplicity in your life, the words of these ancient philosophers and illustrious literary figures throughout the ages will be helpful to you. In fact, it is my hope that we can all take heed and start to make the changes we need to live more fulfilling lives. After all, that is our goal here!

I hope, like me, you will be amazed at how far-reaching and deep their thoughts on simplicity went. These people were advocates of using everything in their life well. Many great thinkers certainly were advocates of simple living, which almost makes them appear to have been clairvoyant, as if they could see where society would be heading in the future. But even more than that, I think they were acutely tuned into mankind's strengths and foibles, and that surely hasn't changed over time.

When exactly did our culture begin straying away from simplicity? The answer could be anyone's guess. All I know is that we have been on an ongoing march toward an unsustainable, overly complex lifestyle. The pursuit of the almighty dollar appears to have become the basis of U.S. civilization, and civility erodes.

Do you remember when life started to get complicated for you and your family? Was it when, like so many people, you bought into the idea that you or your children had to have everything everyone else had? You needed to have the latest computers, cell phones, iPods, flat-screen TVs, cars, and clothes, or your career became more important than relationships and family. So what was the result of that? Probably a big financial mess and perhaps deep loneliness.

Over the last forty years, we have developed into, if not an unsustainable culture, an unhealthy one. The trend of developing technologies to simplify so much of our everyday lives has really led to opposite results in some areas. The trend that began in the nineteenth century continued at an ever-increasing pace in the twentieth century. Keep in mind how many changes have transpired. This has not been simple for me, and I can only imagine if I was forty years older. How could I make sense of some of the changes that I'm seeing? The century that started with horses, simple automobiles, freighters, and radio ended with luxury sedans, cruise ships, airlines, the space shuttle, TV, and the Internet.

Mass media, telecommunications, and information technology (especially computers, books, public education, and the Internet) made the world's knowledge more widely available to people. How many times have you said to someone, "I don't know the answer to that question. Let me Google it." Or "Wikipedia says ..." Gone are the days of spending hours in a library, chasing down information, or reading a whole newspaper. Americans have come to expect everything immediately. But more pleasure comes to those people who actually have to wait in anticipation before receiving something they want. That is one of the ironies of living during these complex, fast-paced times.

Digital technology, in its early stages of mainstream use in the 1980s and 1990s, was gradually widely accepted by most of the world, though concerns about stress and isolation from the overuse of mobile phones, the Internet, and related technologies remain controversial. Take a close look at these staggering numbers. By 2009, 4.6 billion people globally, or nearly half the world's population, used cell phones, and in 2005, over a billion people worldwide used the Internet. Life has certainly sped up and gotten more detailed, so much so that at times people may begin to feel like they are living in a pressure cooker or, at the very least, as if they can't keep up with all the changes.

We are living in an age of complexities. Yes, every century has seen problems with leadership, financial, and cultural issues. But in this century our lives risk becoming unsustainable, unproductive, and often unfulfilled. In this unique complex world we live in today, our culture needs to hold onto the concept of simplicity, because the pace of life is proceeding even faster and will continue to challenge our every fiber. Our American culture of entitlement could only last so long. Let's face it. It has taken too many resources to last, and it has left out too many people. This shadow of reality casts darkness over our country, which it has not seen since the Great Depression.

If your parents learned to purchase only the necessities they could afford because of living through periods of hard economic times, then you know they remember living through the Great Depression. When that generation had its children, these kids were taught to work hard for everything and not to always question if they were happy. Approximately two generations after the Great Depression came the baby boomers. Boomers were born when everything in America was on the upswing. It was an era of great optimism and rapidly growing prosperity.

When we think of the baby boomer generation, we often think of kids who got cars early, liked rock 'n' roll music, and, oh yes, became the first generation to see credit as a way of life, which also soon became America's way of life. It seems clear that using credit to buy everything led to this sense of immediate gratification. The baby boomers naturally set up the next generation to become conditioned to buying anything they wanted. Is it any wonder that the kids of baby boomers now are often referred to as the entitled generation?

My friend Joanne, who works as a manager at a very successful large personal injury law firm on LaSalle Street in Chicago, is always recounting some of her dealings with the young people she manages. She laughs at how overly privileged they act and how often some of them begrudge doing a job that they deem below their expertise. When she explains to them that perhaps they should finish their work on that master's degree they are always talking about, that usually calms them down. Sometimes she says she wants to scream, seeing how they think everything is owed to them. They spend money they can't afford on the latest fashions, and then they do nothing but complain about how they need to make more money. I see this as an example of where this generation's parents perhaps didn't fully communicate to their kids just how tough it can be in the working world. That is why they call it work and they pay you, and yes, it is not always fun! Knowing how much money they are making, Joanne says that when she hears the young people talk about their debt, she feels like they haven't woken up yet to the fact that their lives will continue to be strangled if they don't change their ways.

Here's a little background on how Americans slowly adapted to the concept of debt. Over one hundred years ago, most people who could afford it signed a mortgage to purchase their home or property. Credit was only used for necessities, such as purchasing homes or property. Today people are advised that the purchase price of their home should be no more than three times their annual household income. Keep in mind that on top of your mortgage payments there are property taxes, insurance, upkeep, etc., with interest rates typically 5 to 6 percent. Most of us are unable to live as relaxing a life as our great grandparents, grandparents, or even our parents were able to. Americans did not like to carry large debt in "the old days." So while your grandparents paid off their mortgage, their next greatest expense was the family's food and utility bills. Today, our next greatest expenses are our car payments, credit card debt, Internet and cell phone bills, and cable bills. And like our parents and grandparents, there still is a need for food and utilities.

By the midcentury point, America's memory of the pain felt from the Great Depression was growing foggier. America was on the upswing and, in general, life was good following World War II and the Korean War. That memory grew fainter, and this gave birth to the credit generation. That was my generation, the baby boomers. We are the group that always thought life was good just as long as we had a credit card in hand.

My generation's only knowledge of the Great Depression came from books and movies, such as *It's a*

Wonderful Life. Never again did Americans believe we could or would have to experience an economic shock of the magnitude of that Wall Street Crash of 1929. We were able to adapt very well to lines of credit. We became so comfortable with it that if we liked something, we bought it, regardless of whether we could afford it. Keep in mind how quickly this change came. It was this generation's parents who believed all that mattered when making a purchase was whether you needed it and you could afford to pay cash for it. Remember Visa and MasterCard credit card offers arriving in the mail every day? We actually needed only one credit card, but these corporations were dead set on keeping people buying stuff, regardless of whether we should or not. This is exactly what led to America's recent personal debt implosion, which caught so many Americans in a stranglehold. These situations are virtually inescapable.

Chapter 8
The New America: Pinching Pennies

We make a living by what we get, but we make a life by what we give.
—Winston Churchill

Although many of us saw the hits our bank accounts were taking in the past few years, we never really wanted to adjust our lifestyles to the new reality. In fact, I think we just thought that pretending our economy would continue to go gangbusters forever was the way to deal with it. With blind optimism, we watched things get out of control and didn't do anything about it. I, for one, wondered why we tolerated that now-famous housing bubble as long as we did. We saw it coming for years; the pundits talked about it. Yet, we really didn't do anything about it. Like most optimistic Americans, I wasn't fully aware of the mess that was coming. But like so many others, I enjoyed thinking my house was worth much more than I paid. (Err … you were right, Dad.)

Only simplification can help us make sense of the turmoil we sustained during this last decade. First, employment seemed like the big problem. Next, millions began losing not only their jobs but in some cases, also their homes. One minute many of us thought our homes were worth beaucoup bucks. The next minute we saw the values tumble across the country. People panicked as the values of homes dropped. Where was their extra money going to come from, especially if they lost their job? We became much more aware of some of our wasteful spending. While many American workers continued working, a new attitude of fright developed. Everyone was concerned that possibly their job could be the next to go. Especially if you were nearing the age of retirement but financially not yet ready for it, your fear of losing your job preoccupied most of your thoughts. Your plans for the future drastically changed as you contemplated having to work another ten years. Sometimes it is still hard to believe that our country is fighting not one, not two, but now three economy-sapping wars. However you feel about the reasons for the wars, our government began running up a huge trillion-dollar debt that has made our country a slave to paying off this enormous obligation for years to come. Americans are sorely conscious of the life-changing alterations to our financial futures, as we are forced to figure out new ways to survive.

Think about some of the problems facing different states that are nearly bankrupt—like Illinois, California, Utah, and Wisconsin. Heck, how about the U.S. government? None of us probably ever imagined these kinds of problems could materialize. Were state legislators irresponsible? In some cases, they probably were. But I also think it illustrated how over the top our nation was living.

We believed that we should get things we need when we need them and worried about how to pay for it another day. The only problem is that the day does come, and when there is no money, well, as we all know, it is not a pretty picture. Americans have long relied on the stability of our local and federal government. Acknowledging the fact that your local town or city is having budget problems is one thing, but when you can no longer turn to the state because it doesn't have the funds either, you begin seeing the scary extent of our country's problems. Seeing our federal government having horrendous financial problems really scared us. *What do you mean we don't have any money? We're the United States of America!* Folks, all I can say about this is that if these crises haven't been enough for you to see the importance of starting a Simplicity Revolution to turn things around at all levels of our society, then you *still* aren't paying attention. I'm hoping things like this book can wake us up!

Whenever I hear people complain about having to pay higher taxes, I say to them, "Perhaps think of taxes as another word for 'civilization.' If taxes are what it takes to keep our community's police and fire departments going strong and our libraries open, perhaps higher taxes are the answer." Then I ask them, "How many people do you think would stop for a red light if they weren't worried about the police ticketing them? And how many times have you resented your tax bill when you had to call the firehouse to report a fire or you needed an ambulance sent to your home?" Put simply, there is a cost for living in a highly civilized society, and there truly is no such thing as a free lunch.

Watching what was happening in our economy, were you as surprised as I was to see that people were still shopping at these large retail stores? In fact, many retail stores did not originally take a big hit in sales. Primarily, because people like to shop and they like doing it a lot. In fact, many have turned shopping into a sort of hobby. It certainly provides a sense of adventure for some people. It is common today for people of all races and income levels to plan their day around shopping, not necessarily for anything in particular, but just to be out looking at *stuff*. We all can identify with that excitement, knowing that at any time you might hit upon your quarry—your source of whatever turns you on. Traditionally, big department stores could always count on us to come in and buy. However, as of December 2010, that is no longer the case. Retailers had to simplify by making purchases even more attractive with deep discounts and hope that when the economy improves, shopping prices can return to their higher margin prices.

According to a *New York Times* article from May 2009 (www.nytimes.com/2009/05/02/business/02dollar. html), in today's world, the nation's dollar stores, those once-dowdy chains that lured shoppers by selling some or all of their merchandise for $1, are suddenly hot. They are busily opening new stores, outfitting existing stores with refrigerators and freezers, and sprucing up their aisles with better lighting, fresh paint and new signs.

And while most big retail chains are closing stores and radically cutting back on new outlets, the Dollar chains are planning to open hundreds of stores this year in some of the best locations to which they have ever had access.

Dollar stores have long had a reputation for being down-at-the-heels places to buy cheap, generic goods. Now, while keeping their low prices, they are revamping their image and climbing the respectability ladder. That is why shoppers—who are now looking for cheaper brands of paper towels, toilet paper, wrapping paper, greeting cards, decorations, and cleaning materials—have discovered this new type of store. I say "new" only because, prior to this economic downturn, people thought of these stores as being shopped by only poor people, while the middle class and wealthy shoppers turned to buying these types of products at Walmart and Target. Now, all types of shoppers are looking to save more money and are frequenting stores, like Dollar Tree and the Dollar Store. It is evident that every dollar a person can save is extremely important in today's economy.

Here is a recent story I'm still laughing about. Driving home from a shopping trip at my nearby Target store, I recalled that I would be passing near a Dollar Tree store. I remembered that *Times* article and thought, *Heck, I need to save money. I should check it out.* Talking about "stuff," this store had tons of it, some of it useful and some, well, not so useful. After cruising around the store, I found some lightbulbs for one dollar and some tape, put them in my basket, and my shopping was done. Walking out of the store, I saw a camera tripod set up next to my car. As I put my key into the door, out of nowhere, this news reporter and cameraman approached me and said, "We saw you walking out of the Dollar Tree store and would like to interview you about your shopping experience." I'll admit that my initial reaction was to give a flat out "No."

All I could imagine was people who knew me as a career person, who I had employed in the past, would see me on the nightly news and think, *Poor Sue, she must really have hit some hard times in life.* Then, luckily, my better self-emerged, and I realized that if I was going to write about middle-class people shopping in these types of stores, of course I had to let them interview me. Who doesn't want to value shop? Honestly, I can't think of a better store to shop value. If you have one near you, and especially if you have small children, they really are worth checking out.

It didn't happen immediately, but about five days later the story ran. People I didn't even know, like the lady who checks member cards at my local YMCA, said to me, "I saw you on the news last night!" Another woman walking by her looked at my husband and me and said, "Oh yes, I saw you too!" For one fleeting moment I was a TV star at my local Y, where everyone now knew I shop at dollar stores. And that is all the unpaid advertising I am doling out about that subject. Just to be clear, living a simple life does not mean you have to give up wearing makeup, ladies. The only embarrassment I felt about that interview was that I had gone out that day without any makeup and looked a complete mess—on TV!

As Al Gore said in his book, *The Assault on Reason*, a well-connected citizenry is made up of men and women who discuss and debate ideas. Therefore, it is my hope that if you have a social network or book group, you can discuss some of what I am offering up for discussion. I hope to inspire a return of sanity to our American lives by urging people to live simpler and more peaceful lifestyles so that they can remember, even when their wallets are almost empty, just how sweet life really is. By discussing some of the ideas contained in this book, not only can it help each individual get the message, but it can also help your local community contend with some of the problems it currently is facing.

You will find that I don't try to list every single way to make your life simpler, because I assume each of you is unique and can search for what will work best in your own life. However, I do put forward many suggestions, some of which you will want to incorporate into your everyday life. Like any art form, practicing simplicity in life takes exactly that: practice. And everyone's idea of simplicity is unique; one person's simple lifestyle might seem decadent to one observer and impossibly austere to another. Perhaps this is why it is called a person's personal life path. Some people love mountain climbing. Ask these people why they climb mountains, and you'll probably get as many answers as there are climbers. I myself would reply, "Because I didn't know there was a way to avoid that ridiculously steep climb." My point is that the options we have for finding simplicity depend on the life path we choose.

Always remember the future belongs to those who believe in their dreams. Perhaps our culture did have to change. But change doesn't have to scare us. We've always been good at doing it. Let's admit it. Our culture had gotten a bit bloated, and we'd developed some lazy tendencies. But now we have a new challenge ready for us to explore and improve upon. I think some amazing things lay not too far off in the future for America. Hopefully, you're feeling this way also.

Chapter 9
Curbing Your Thirst for Stuff

Simplicity, clarity, singleness: these are the attributes that give our lives power and vividness and joy.

—Richard Halloway

I enjoy reading Friedrich Nietzsche, a nineteenth-century German philosopher, probably because of his contrarian opinions and ways. Nietzsche understood that the success of a person's life wasn't about those things he collected along the way, but about one's ethics and kindness toward others. In today's world, how many people get their self-esteem or meaning of life through the things they purchase along the way? I would venture to say too many. Like Nietzsche, who lived during the rise of European materialism and developed an antimaterialistic philosophy, I'm optimistic that a Simplicity Revolution could be ignited here in America and result in many upsides for our society and culture, much as it did for Nietzsche. I highly recommend finding a moment to read closely some of Nietzsche's works, especially during this difficult economic period our country is experiencing.

Don't you think that people actually long for an escape from the heightened anxiety born in this age of information overload? Let's face it. We are exhausted from constantly having to manage our time and resources. Many problems have no easy answers, but once the problems are confronted, life can get simpler, easier. Also, you may find more satisfaction by simply allowing things to be. Our culture has made many people think that the grass is always greener on the other side of the hill, leaving some people to feel that they do not have enough. Ask yourself what will ultimately fulfill you? Is it having more children? Is it making vice president at your company? Is it writing a book? We all have dreams for ourselves, and that is where the magic of life comes into play.

Curbing your thirst for "stuff" is where your life begins to take shape, because it speaks to your values. Without going through all of the environmental reasons that so many people are now choosing this path and getting by with far less than just a decade before, I hope you can understand how we as American consumers need to at least turn into a reusable society ASAP. We need to learn how to get the most out of something we previously purchased before we cast it aside. Don't you think we already have too many waste dumps in our country, too many Mount Trashmores?

Adopting a reusable lifestyle allows us to have more time to invest in our relationships with spouses, children, friends, neighbors, and coworkers. Why? Because collecting all of the "stuff" we think we need in our households requires someone in that household to be working hard to pay for that "stuff." Next, somebody needs to find a place to put it, maintain it, and one day spends time and maybe even money to get rid of it! And as for the time spent buying your "stuff," could it have been better spent perhaps helping your aging parents or a neighbor?

Imagine if we could develop an anti-materialistic philosophy, like Nietzsche wrote about—simplicity one person at a time. Perhaps we could redirect some of our time, or at least use it more wisely, and begin to teach young people that the "supersize me" culture of the last two decades was not healthy for our bodies and definitely not for our planet. Let's try to show new respect for what we already have. If you allow this book to aid you in your lifestyle of awareness, then in due course, you should gain a greater sense of control over your own life. And soon you will be on your way to advancing a Simplicity Revolution throughout our country. Only you can decide how far to go with this concept in your own life. But we better all hope that people around the world will start listening, because I believe that our planet over the last few years has been giving us warnings that we have abused it for too long, and it can't continue in this manner.

If there is one thing that everyone should be learning from this economic downturn, it is that just because you like something does not mean you should buy it. If you like something but cannot afford to pay cash to purchase it, then any reasonable person should understand that you do not purchase it. It's an old rule but 100 percent "on the mark." It sounds so simple, but it is not. This is something that will take self-examination and decision making.

Stand in a store and envision the end of the month when all of your bills are due. Does that new jacket on the rack still look great? Will it be worth overextending yourself and paying for it over several months? Do you love it that much? Or is that nice *old* jacket at home starting to look good to you again? How do you feel as you think about adding to your debt because of the new jacket? Don't you feel better picturing yourself *not* having to pay for the jacket? Wouldn't it be fun to be free at the end of the month rather than struggle to make the payment on something that you did not absolutely need?

If you can't stand having to wear items that are many seasons out of style, check some of the resale shops and find something unique for very little money. How does that idea suit you? Of course, ultimately, the decision is yours. But work through it before going forward. Perhaps the vision of your money sitting in your nest egg will win out, and so will you!

A Generation's Marker

Every generation has a marker, an event or trend with which it becomes associated. In the twentieth century, first we had the Lost Generation (World War I), and then we had the Greatest Generation (1901 to 1924), followed by the Silent Generation, the children of the Great Depression (1925 to 1945). A population explosion known as the Baby Boom Generation (1946 to 1964) followed the return of World War II veterans. Next came Generation X, loosely defined as those born from roughly 1965 to 1976, followed by Generation Y (also known as the millennial, or echo, boomers). The broadest definition of this group generally includes those born from 1977 to 2002. Then along came Generation Z, also known as Generation I, for the Internet Generation (1990 to 2005). This generation is also dubbed "the digital natives," because it is obsessed with iPod, iTunes, iPhone, iPad, iBook, and Facebook. Gone are the days of e-mail, e-book, and eBay. It's all about "I" now. (By some fluke, YouTube, the pioneer of the broadcast-yourself industry, wasn't named iTube).

Not having experienced such a major downturn in its economy since the Great Depression, America refers to this hard economic period as the Great Recession. Christened by many economists as "the new normal," it is forcing all generations to change their life's expectations from high-paying salaried jobs to just being able to find a job. Therefore, I have tagged this generation coming of age during this period in American history the "Bootstrap Generation," because many of them will be required to pull themselves up by their own bootstraps as traditional social support systems continue to vanish.

Today's New World

All the above titles can be confusing, let's face it. It is in that confusion, however, that today's complex new world is reflected. Sociologists are predicting that what I call today's "Bootstrap Generation" will grow up knowing how to live simpler lives than recent previous generations. And when they settle into family life, they will put that ahead of their work and corporate status, earlier than the last two previous generations. In general, they are also trying to live healthier lifestyles. According to

Vegetarian Times, 7.3 million people in this country follow a vegetarian-based diet. And approximately 0.5 percent, or 1 million, of those are vegans, who consume no animal products at all. In addition, 10 percent of U.S. adults, or 22.8 million people, say they largely follow a vegetarian-inclined diet. So although we talked about others doing it, we now are truly choosing to eat that way more and more. This trend is expected to continue, as witnessed by the growing number of vegetarians and vegans in our midst and the availability of vegetarian menus at restaurants and even fast-food places. I look at this as Americans taking a simpler approach to what and how they are choosing to eat. In the sixties, there was nothing more appealing than going to a restaurant for a steak dinner. Today, that doesn't sound as appealing as it once did. The simple truth is that our taste and knowledge about the food we eat has changed dramatically and probably for the better.

Many people are also trading in those large gas-guzzling SUVs for smaller cars and hybrid vehicles because they are growing more environmentally conscious about the carbon footprint they will leave behind than generations before them. Hummers and the like are taking a backseat to smaller, more energy-efficient cars. This can only be good news for the environment.

There is another interesting change in today's world: Our youth, according to *Chicago Tribune* writer Ted Gregory, are now the most tolerant generation in history. The Pew Research Center conducted an extensive study of teens and twenty-something's, showing that members of the Millennial Generation, born between 1981 and 2000, are more radically tolerant than their elders. The study goes on to report that nearly six in ten millennials say immigrants strengthen our country, compared with 43 percent of adults aged thirty or older.

Have you ever wondered why we work ourselves into a sweat, week in and week out, only to find ourselves feeling overstressed, overweight, and overworked? I did and learned that in the "up" economy, according to psychologists, people were successful, but in many cases, they were missing too much of their lives.

I hope you will learn there is a need to pause to examine your life and take a Simplicity Revolution to heart. I believe that to do so will radically alter the way you live, and the quality of your life ultimately will get better. I sincerely believe that simplicity will ultimately prove to be the silver lining found in this Great Recession, revealing that an economic pause was a necessary interlude on our path to a saner, happier lifestyle.

Chapter 10
Avoiding the Debt Treadmill
(aka the Hamster Wheel)

Nature is pleased with simplicity.
—Isaac Newton

To ease yourself into a simpler life, try saying this to yourself as a mantra: *Use up, wear out, make do, or do without.*

Next, remember your goal is to simplify your life, so when faced with the temptation to add something new to it, ask yourself these six simple, clarifying questions, and answer them honestly:

1. Do I love it?
2. Do I need it?
3. Can I live without it?
4. How will I feel if I buy it/don't buy it today?
5. Can I pay for it now?
6. Where will I put it?

If you answer the above questions honestly, you will find yourself walking away more frequently from the elements that can complicate your life. From coast to coast, we're moving from conspicuous consumption—buying without regard—to calculated consumption, according to Marshal Cohen, an analyst at the NPD Group, the retailing research and consulting firm.

As you strive to become more conscious in the way you live your life, you will find that rethinking what you believe is necessary and leads to incredibly satisfying results. When a person is surrounded by an abundance of wealth, information, distractions, tools, and services, it can become easy to start thinking that all of these things are truly vital. While some of them may be vital, most are not. Figuring out what is truly required to do your best work, or be your best self, is what living consciously is all about.

Amid this weak job and housing market, consumers are saving more and spending less than they have in decades, and industry professionals expect that trend to continue. Consumers saved 6.4 percent of their after-tax income in June 2010, suggesting that as dependent as the American economy is on shoppers, it will be less likely that shoppers will be opening their wallets and purses as frequently as in the boom days. Consumer spending and personal incomes were essentially flat compared with levels prior to the Great Recession. And this sort of spending change is anticipated to stay with us for many years to come.

Sometimes it feels like we are at the mercy of big corporations and their marketing machines. The more they say we need something, the more we begin to think we do. I know I have been a willing victim in purchasing many new items. Did I really need to purchase them at all? No. Could I have found the exact same item used and recycled for my purposes? Yes.

You can painlessly regain control over your life once you make a commitment to curbing your addiction to purchasing "stuff." As Americans, we have grown up groomed to desire more and better "stuff." Breaking those habits of running out to buy something new, even while an old item is still being paid off, really will not be that difficult once you begin living more conscientiously and acting responsibly when it comes to how you spend your money.

I have long believed that our approach to purchasing items, as if they are temporary, is flawed. When things break or rip, many of us just dispose of them. In the past, people actually took a moment out of their lives to determine whether something could be fixed or sewed. If this is something you can relate to, or if you are the kind of person who is always wondering why your life has gotten so complicated with so much credit card debt, I hope you will agree that we need to become more of a reusable society again. A reusable society is one where people know how to sew and fix things. Remember when people took shoes to be repaired at a shoemaker? Or when people sewed a torn jacket, rather than retired it? We even darned the holes in our socks, for heaven's sake.

Do you remember when people did many of their own home repairs? If you do, you probably are a baby boomer or older. This is not to say that nobody in America today knows how to work around the house; it is just that a majority of Americans, whether they can afford it or not, don't stop and think twice about paying someone else to do something they could possibly do themselves. Not long ago, people knew how to get the most out of something before it was cast aside or thrown out. Also, we took great pride in being able to do things for ourselves rather than paying for everything to be done for us. Drive down your street on "garbage night" in your neighborhood, and you'll likely see this is no longer true. Nobody wants to fix anything anymore. It's easier to just replace something rather than fix it.

A New American Lifestyle Begins to Emerge

By 2010, as America's thirst for "stuff" began to diminish, we started seeing new trends. According to retailers and analysts, consumers began gravitating more toward experiences than possessions, opting to use their extra cash for nights at home with family, watching movies, and playing games—or for "staycations" in the backyard. Many retailing professionals think this is not a fad, but rather are calling this "the new normal."

In a *New York Times* article, Jennifer Black, president of the retailing research company Jennifer Black & Associates and a member of the Governor's Council of Economic Advisors in Oregon, recently said, "I think many of these changes are permanent changes. I think people are realizing they don't need what they had. They're more interested in creating memories."

She largely attributes this to baby boomers' continuing concerns about the job market and their ability to send their children to college. "While they will still spend, they will spend less and differently," she said. "It appears that people have to reset their priorities, or maybe we can say we are coming down to where we ought to be in order to pull simplicity into our lives."

Anyone who owes more money than he has is running endlessly on the debt treadmill. Like a hamster running on its wheel, with no beginning and no end, the person is trapped in a circle of debt, with no way out. The person runs around and around on the debt wheel, going nowhere except into more debt. Interest charges ensure that the person will not escape his or her predicament.

By purchasing goods before you have earned them, you are in effect borrowing from the future to pay for the present. It's the exact opposite of saving or investing, because you are the one paying interest on credit debt, rather than the bank paying you.

Interest rates on credit cards are typically much higher than savings rates and even higher than many alternative investments (like stocks, bonds, or CDs). By carrying big balances on credit cards, people can begin to feel that they are hopeless in paying them off, so their balances continue to rise. Remember that every bit you pay down makes it easier to pay the rest down. Once you get into credit card debt, you fall further and further behind, because in addition to funding current expenditures, you also need to pay for the previous expenditures that are already on your credit card.

The more I looked deeply into our lifestyles in America, the clearer it became. The debt treadmills on which so many of us are walking are due in large part to our own self-condemnation. The "work hard, play hard" concept, which I bought into early on, really was a well–thought-out marketing concept that encouraged the poor, the middle class, and the rich to think that the key to happiness was spending money on those big-ticket or frequently desired items, such as beauty products, clothes, a new sailboat, a bigger car, etc. After all, this was a surefire way to prove to your family and friends just how hard you worked to deserve your new toys and how very deserving you are. In today's economy, many of us cannot survive without our credit cards because we cannot afford even life's basic necessities without them. This is especially true for those of us who already had large debts when the Great Recession hit.

How to Begin Getting Yourself Out of Debt

I think it's safe to say that we are witnessing a new day dawning across the country. Many Americans are recognizing the importance of jumping off the debt wheel. If you are already in credit card debt, don't worry. Follow some of these recommendations to get yourself out of debt. Believe me, life will feel much simpler.

- Never forget that steadily paying down a small portion helps. The more you pay down, the easier it is to pay the rest, because there is less interest due each month. Of course, this assumes you don't keep running up the card with new purchases. Remember to ask yourself the six questions above and you will find yourself purchasing less and less unnecessary "stuff."

- If possible, pay more each month on your credit card than what you spend on your credit card.

- Start paying for your purchases in cash when you have the money.

- Never lose sight of the big picture. It's often discouraging because it seems like it will take forever to get out of credit card debt. Just think how much simpler your life will be without that credit card payment hanging over you at the end of each month.

- If your credit card rates are high, call your lender and ask them to reduce the rate. You'd be surprised. I've heard of companies reducing their rates from as much as 18 percent to as low as 7 to 9 percent.

  Clearly, paying off debt on a house or piece of property is one thing. Ultimately, you should get some of your money back once you sell that property. Then again, store-bought items usually are worth much less the minute you leave the store. These items might make you feel good for a while, but in the long run you are losing money on them. Are they really worth it? Be careful saying yes!

Always remember that carrying tons of debt complicates life and stresses you out. Get off that treadmill, and you will be able to handle other stressors much better, feel happier, and breathe more easily. I guarantee the world will seem to be a much happier place.

The Nest Egg

When I was young, I had a friend who taught me two things. Jack, a quite successful young businessman (at least by my very young standards), told me that people needed to create a nest egg for themselves. This nest egg, he explained, would literally give people the ability to drop some money into a smart investment, should the opportunity present itself. And he was correct. I was able to buy my first home on my own before I turned thirty.

The next thing I learned from Jack was that everyone needs to have "screw-you money" set aside. Perhaps Jack's words were a little more salty than that, but I'm sure you get their meaning. Jack's message was that if your employer is not treating you right, you always have to maintain your ability to walk out and find another employer who will treat you well. Granted, moving between jobs in today's job market is harder, but this is still something worthwhile to remember. Knowing you could lose your job at any time certainly should be enough to encourage you to not play so lightly with your credit cards.

The "Pay Now" or "Pay Later" Question

One thing that many Americans would agree with is that they don't like paying high prices—the cheaper the better, whether food, gasoline, utilities, etc. We want to believe that we are obtaining the best price on items we purchase, while the rest of the world—well, they just have to pay those high prices.

Unlike in most other countries, Americans have long pretended that the low cost of gasoline was because we deserved it that way. We were not like those silly Canadians and Europeans who paid double what we paid for one gallon of gasoline. I guess we thought it was our God-given right. In fact, because our gas costs so much less, most Americans drive their cars way too much. We drive far more than people in other countries, and we continue to be the worst offenders concerning global environmental pollution. Yet, will you ever hear a politician or government official suggest our gas prices need to be raised in balance with the rest of the world? I don't think so! For one thing, most politicians throughout our country actually like their jobs, and they know this would likely be the end of them. I guess it is just easier to face this building global warming crisis than face the shame of losing a seat in Congress. What about the shame of allowing our nation to put future generations' lives in jeopardy?

Another thing to remember when you think of the "pay now" or "pay later" question is just how simple it would be for you to adopt a reusable lifestyle. We work hard as young adults, building careers, relationships, and families, only to find that we really have far too little time to offer anyone, including ourselves. Have you ever driven past one of those beautiful sailboat harbors on a gorgeous day and wondered why there are so many boats just sitting tied up dockside? Or why is your neighbor's lovely summer home on the lake seldom used? The answer probably is that the owners are too busy working to maintain these wonderful things. Thus, many people often don't have the time to enjoy them. So again I say pay now or pay later, because if you bring upon yourself enormous stresses without taking time to decompress, the cost to you may result in more than you want to lose.

That Marvelous Credit/Debit Card

Credit. *Ah, yes!* It worked for a while, but then we got stuck in a cycle of debt. Once in—I cannot repeat this enough—once in, it is just not an easy place to get out of. It's sort of like the seven circles of hell in Dante's Inferno. Pulling out that credit/debit card is very easy. In fact, it is too easy. But paying your bill at the end of the month, well, that's downright painful.

As I said earlier, clean living is best defined as minimal, plain, effortless, and directly opposite to how American lifestyles have evolved over the last few decades. I repeat, I am not an economist, but I do feel that clean living moved out of our lives once credit cards moved into our wallets. Credit instigated the fast pace of our lifestyles, because we could purchase more of everything sooner. Never wanting to miss a challenge, Americans showed that they knew how to use credit well, and once the hook was set, we could not spit it out.

Living on credit felt so good, but only for a short while. Once we got trapped in our own self-created cycle of debt, our lives just became more complicated. The "pay now" or "pay later" question is a valuable lesson to keep in mind for everything—and not just for today, but every day of your life. Hopefully, it eventually will result in allowing you to live a more complete, untainted, and simple life. As we have found, slewing our way through debt is not a lesson to pass on to our progeny. What happened to us in 2008 we now know should have been called the Great

American Implosion of Personal Debt! Once around this slough is surely enough for anyone.

Most people may remember a time when, if you couldn't own your car outright in three years, you didn't buy one. It is quite common for people to not hesitate and purchase a long-term credit line on a car. Today, people will purchase cars, knowing they will not be paid off for up to 138 months. Looking at the interest on that lien, doesn't it make you question why Americans wouldn't opt for taking public transportation, which is available in so many locales? And why aren't Americans screaming for good public transportation in all communities? Yet, more cars continue moving throughout our cities. We have to face it, we Americans love our cars.

If your debit or credit card is making it too easy to buy things, perhaps you need to try carrying cash once again. When you need to actually start peeling those twenties out of your wallet to make a purchase, it hurts a little more than when you just swipe that card. The banks have been so smart at sucking us into every program they can think of to entice us into debt. The debit card has removed our sense of it being real money we are about to spend. Do not fall for it. In fact, you know those checks they send us all the time, which make it look so easy for you to get a little extra cash? Immediately cut those up and place them in your garbage can. Those are just another attempt to get you on that debt treadmill that pays the banks such wonderful interest.

What You Should Have Learned From This Economic Cleansing Period

If there is one thing that everyone should have learned from the Great Recession it is that the economy can be fickle, so always be prepared should a downturn happen again. If you like something but cannot afford to pay cash for it, do not purchase it. Just think toward the end of the month when all of your bills will be due. Does that new jacket still look so great? Won't your jacket at home still keep you as warm as it did last winter? Maybe you could check some of the resale shops and find something for a less expensive price. In fact, I know you could. Some of my smartest clothes purchases have come from resale shops. There is nothing more satisfying than showing up to a big event where you know all of the women have shopped at expensive boutiques for their clothing, and you are getting so much attention for your outfit, which cost a wise total of $11.99. Now, that is fun. That is *really* fun!

Ultimately, the decision is yours. Remember, the money you would spend on clothes, an additional car, etc., would probably do you better sitting in the nest egg that you're trying to build than in your closet or garage.

Now Begin to Save Money

At times in this economy it can feel like you are hanging onto the side of a cliff by your fingernails. Watching so many millions of people losing jobs across our country has made even the most formerly secure employee take note of the situation and perhaps even begin giving thanks for a job he or she earlier disdained. How can you be prepared for the worst? Living simply with your money—in other words, living cautiously—really can pay off. When a person loses a job or can't find one in the predicted time frame, it is amazing how fast money goes out when none is coming in. This is why I want to encourage everyone to stay prepared. Remember to always have that nest egg set aside. This is exactly what it is for. Unfortunately, life doesn't always play out the way we like, and sometimes we're faced with unexpected financial emergencies during the course of our lives. That is why it is important for each person, whether we live simply or not, to know the approximate amount of money it takes to live each month. It is only then that we can budget whatever money we have to work with.

Simplify and Modify Your Lifestyle

Learning to live modestly simplifies our lives and takes much of the pressure off. Never mind beating yourself up for past waste (that's a waste of energy in itself). Just start by thinking about what you've been spending and what you might need that money for in the future—like food or medical care. Think about how much you already have and whether you actually have to spend any more money for a while. Maybe it's time for a spending break. You'll probably be surprised at how much extra money you can scrape up over a month if you just watch the spending. Modest adjustments can simplify your life by removing bits of debt and providing you a tad of a cushion.

Figure out what it takes to live modestly for a month. You'll need to cover your regular bills, such as mortgage or rent, utilities (gas, electric, telephone), car payment and gas for work, food, etc.

Once you think you've got the bare bones covered, look at how much cash you think you'll have to spend. Planning to spend $600 this month on everything from groceries to gas to your sister's birthday present? Cut that in half and challenge yourself to live on less.

The Simple Power of Saving

Before you throw your hands up and say, "Ridiculous," just try it. There's no failure here. It's an experiment. It's to see if it can be done. After all, even if you miss by $150, you've still spent much less than you thought was possible. Hit the mark and you've got money in the bank and fewer complications in your life. How much could you save every year if you decided to live modestly? How much less stuff would you have? How much happier and less stressed-out would you be?

Let me illustrate: Save just $200 a month by living modestly, put it in a Roth IRA earning an average of 5 percent, reinvest your tax refund, and in twenty-five years you'll have $90,000. Save $300 a month and you'd have $134,000. Save $500 a month and you'd have $224,000. *Now that's a grand slam!* Is twenty-five years too far off for you, given your age? I'll address later on things you can do now to benefit financially and psychologically, simple changes over the next couple of years. Believe me, I am no economic genius, like Suze Orman, I'm just trying to kick things off for you here.

Living a simple lifestyle usually means battling the influences and motivations to spend that come every day from advertising, friends, shopping at the mall, and other temptations. It often means taking a little more time to distinguish between what you want and what you need before you buy it. And it means being willing to accept that what you already have is good enough. The Dalai Lama also says, "If a person confronts one's problems head on, he will be in a better position to appreciate the depth and nature of a problem." If your problem has been overspending, the next part of this book should help you to figure out the impact that this problem is having on your life.

Now we come to that really fun part of the book where I try to convince everybody to learn at least an infinitesimal amount about how to budget those monthly expenses. As this is a book on simplicity, I am going to attempt to keep this explanation as simple as possible. The only people who should skip these next paragraphs are those of you who are either financial wizards or those who are anticipating a lottery or gold strike in the near future.

The first thing to understand is the difference between your financial goals and those financial dreams you harbor for your future; they are definitely not the same. A dream is exactly what the word means; it is something you hope for. Your financial goal is something you can actually achieve and plan for. In fact, it is setting these goals, taking into account your own financial reality, which makes your dreams possible.

Your financial goal should state:
• what you plan to accomplish;

- what resources you'll need to make it happen;
- how much time you'll need to make it happen; and
- how you plan to make your goal fit into your overall budget and life.

Did you know that when setting up a basic budget, you should make sure your monthly expenses follow these recommended percentages of your net paycheck: housing (35 percent); debt (15 percent); general living, such as food, clothing, and utilities (25 percent); transportation (15 percent); and savings (10 percent).

List your financial goals. First, place your short-term goals that are achievable in the near future. Then list your medium-term and long-term goals that will take more than a year to accomplish.

1. **Estimate the cost.** How much money do you think it will take to reach each goal? Create the estimate, and write the resulting figure under the "Estimated Cost" category.

2. **Set a target date.** When do you hope or need to meet your goals? Set a target date for each goal on your list, and use this as your deadline to meet or beat.

3. **Determine how much money you need to save in order to accomplish the goal.** Divide the estimated cost of your first goal by the number of weeks until your target date. This will show you how much money you need to save each week to meet your goal. Enter the resulting figure in the "Amount to Save

Weekly" column, and repeat for all of the other goals that you've listed.

4. **Budget for your goals.** Rework your budget to include the money you need to meet your goals. Decide where you can cut back in order to find "new" money. Then put your plan into action, and watch those financial goals turn into financial reality!

5. **Be realistic** about how much time and money it will take to reach each goal.

6. **Keep motivated** by regularly visiting your list to check on your progress.

7. **Setbacks will happen.** If something throws you off of your target date, don't suspend your plan. Immediately set a new date.

8. **Do you have more goals than you can work on at once?** Determine which ones are most important, and make those your first priority.

9. **Not sure where all of your money goes each month?** Track your spending with this worksheet, and solve the mystery once and for all.

10. **The smartest first step in managing any cash that does come your way** is to always pay off high-interest debt, like credit cards. Hopefully you will get into a position where all of your debt is paid off. If that is the case, take the next big step: consider working with your local bank's investment services representative to establish an emergency fund by gradually setting aside money in a money

market account, where you can park your money while it collects interest.

EXPENSES	Week 1	Week 2	Week 3	Week 4	Week 5
Groceries					
Household cleaning supplies, home repairs, etc.					
Cars gas, car repairs, maintenance, etc.					
Clothing and Personal Care haircuts, beauty products, etc.					
Entertainment eating out, coffee shops, movies, books, magazines, concerts, hobbies, etc.					

Medical insurance, etc.				
WEEKLY TOTAL				

Ignoring the "Mega" (Mad) Men

Since the 1950s, Americans have been easily led by TV and radio advertisements and other forms of marketing. Today, everywhere you go around the world, the big corporations have their marketing machines busily attempting to convince us to buy their products. The more the big corporations tell us we need to purchase something, the more we think we do, whether we do or not. Even during the boom times of the 1990s, sociologists and psychologists started to see that people were questioning their quality of life. According to psychologist and author of the book *Flow* Mihaly Csikszentmihalyi, "to be really happy we have to actively create our own experiences, rather than passively let the media and marketers create them for us. When we are content with our lives, consumption loses its appeal."

I recognize when I knowingly have made a needless purchase, yet as anyone can tell you, the worst kind of victim is one who saw it coming and still bought it. Did I really need to purchase another new pair of black jeans, when I already have two pairs? Probably not! Could I have found the exact same item at a resale shop, instead of at Nordstrom?

And Now a Message from Our Sponsor

In March 2010, market intelligence firm comScore surveyed results, reporting a significant decline in brand loyalty since the start of the Great Recession. Less than half of surveyed U.S. consumers reported purchasing the brand they most wanted, down from a whopping 54 percent in March 2008. Since more people than ever are watching how they spend their money, generic brands are now being purchased at an alarming rate compared with the brand-name corporations, such as Nabisco, Kraft, Birds Eye, etc.

What is so worrying to these corporations is how pleased people are with these generic products. Predictions are that consumers will stick with their new generic brands, much to the alarm of some big American corporations.

The whole purpose of big companies is to develop relationships with consumers so they can understand and take advantage of how customers make their purchasing decisions. This helps marketers improve their marketing effectiveness. This long–thought-out plot to trap consumers into buying and into brand loyalty appears to be in jeopardy.

I am going to present to you how you can painlessly regain control over your purchasing power. Stay away from purchasing items that say "New," "Improved," "Ultra soft," or "More absorbent." If it sounds like these words are being used to sell something, that's exactly what they are trying to do. Manufacturers are always looking for new ways to sell consumers on purchasing more of their old products. Have you ever noticed any real improvement made in these "new and improved" products? If so, I would wager it was minimal, if at all. When an older item that is working for you, it probably doesn't stop working just because a newer product comes along. Once the product maker completes running all of its group focus testing, they are able to decide which catchy phrase to attach to the product so it is more likely to end up in your shopping cart. These large corporations may have products you need in your daily life, but stay "real" with your approach to need. Remember you are trying to simplify, so purchase items you can afford. Try using those coupons offered for product introductions, so you can at least compare whether the "new and improved" is either, or both.

For over a year now, I've been watching the U.S. consumers' shift to value purchasing among every day and discretionary goods. Moreover, we are seeing evidence that an economic recovery will not necessarily mean a snap back to the days of footloose spending. So what does this all mean? According to marketing professionals, once people got accustomed to the less expensive generic brands and they were satisfied and saving money at the same time, consumers purchased less of those well-known expensive brand-name goods.

Breaking the habit of running out to buy something new, even while the old stuff is still working fine, will not be that difficult. Once you begin living a more mindful and conscientious lifestyle, you will be surprised at how much of your money you regain. Sometimes, we think of everything we buy as disposable. If this is something you can relate to, or if you are the kind of person who is always wondering why your life has gotten so complicated with so many credit card bills, now is the time to begin curbing your thirst for "stuff." Adopting a reusable lifestyle allows us to have more time to invest in relationships with spouses, children, and friends. Why? Because collecting all of the "stuff" we think we need in our household requires someone in that household to work to pay for that "stuff."

What jumps out at me is the word "thirst." I believe curbing our thirst for "stuff" will give you a renewed sense of respect for what you already have in life, and chances are that there is plenty of "stuff" we could afford sharing with those less fortunate than ourselves.

"New" Doesn't Necessarily Mean Better

Here's my dilemma. I can purchase a simple metal spade for my garden at either Crate and Barrel for $15.95 or my local thrift store for probably a couple of dollars. The Crate and Barrel spade is definitely cuter; it's painted white and has the neatest handle. Then again, just down the street at our local Salvation Army store, my eyes befall this sturdy-looking steel garden spade for seventy-five cents. *Hmm … which do you think I should buy?* If you guessed the garden spade for seventy-five cents, you'd be right.

How many times have you stopped at a store, like a Crate and Barrel or Antique Hardware, and, voilà, you have another $119 on your Visa. Did you really need to spend so much money just because you were having friends over and wanted to serve them out of those darling new salad bowls or dessert cups? You could have purchased nearly the same exact thing at a thrift store for just a few dollars.

Many unique and fun items can be found at thrift stores. From household and garden items, such as eating utensils and chinaware to artwork are normally available. It is also a fun way to show your friends and family how creative you can be while using far less money than if you shopped in a normal department store. Thrift stores can offer you a one-of-a-kind item you weren't even looking for. It is definitely a way to give your home an inexpensive eclectic look, and it's not because you purchased something Crate and Barrel featured on the cover of its new catalog. If anything, I always blushed when friends would start raving over one of my recent finds. They would be so impressed, and it was such an inexpensive item! Whenever I have people over, I love pulling out some of the beautiful, unusual pieces that I've purchased at thrift stores. Shopping at thrift stores allows for me to buy eclectic things very inexpensively. Unfortunately, this became a trap for me, because I really enjoy getting deals. Who doesn't? But, unfortunately for me, buying for the sake of buying resulted in my accumulating too much "stuff" until I finally had to say, "Enough already!" To be honest, maybe my husband said that first.

Be honest with yourself about this question. Are you the type of person who always has to have the latest version of everything? Here is an example that amazed me: I purchased the original Apple 3G iPhone when it first came out. I'll admit it, I was very impressed by what I was seeing on those TV commercials, and I had to have it. I love it. Since that purchase over twenty-six months ago, I have been very happy with my purchase, so happy that I—who never liked talking about any technological gadgets—find myself in conversation often wanting to chat about all of the new applications I have downloaded on my phone. Well, no more than two years have gone by, and there have been two new versions of the iPhone. Did I like the new and improved versions? Absolutely. Did I consider purchasing a new one? Well, no. My 3G iPhone still works great and I still love it. Would it be nice to be able to download some of the newer applications that come with the 4G iPhone? Yes. Could I use those new apps? Definitely! Do I absolutely find those new apps tempting? Well, yes and no. Looking past all of those new cool commercials for the latest version was difficult, but once I thought it through, I was able to avoid spending money on something I really don't need. Now here is the funny part of this story. If I had a dollar for every time a person asked me "Why are you still using the 3G iPhone? You do know a better version has come out," I could take everyone reading this book out for a cup of coffee. Okay, maybe not Starbucks, but coffee nevertheless. I got so tired of people assuming there was something wrong with using the older version of a product. After all, we are in a recession and my phone is hardly two years old. Also, while standing in line at Starbucks, everyone is always chatting away on their cell phones. Occasionally, I'll see people checking out my phone, as if to check out which version of the iPhone I am using. And, of course these are the people who always have the latest upgrade—like I'm so jealous, right?

I'd like to offer up a little info on how to save money

on all kinds of household items as well as clothing. Yes, I was an antique dealer until the economy dried up and I had to close my shop. Antique dealers comb through resale and thrift stores religiously. They know how to identify valuable cast-off gems of all kinds. Depending on what you are looking for, you can find some valuable pieces of china, pottery, glassware, jewelry, and the list goes on and on. There are all kinds of cookery items to be found: cast-iron pans, bakeware, beautiful ceramic mixing bowls, casserole dishes, and vases. You name it, and I've found it.

Antique collectors sometimes get lucky and come up with a really good find, and some of their finds get sold on eBay. I guess the excitement of the antique business is because you never know what your next search is going to turn up. If you are interested in checking it out, I recommend visiting a thrift store with a friend, preferably someone who has an antique mentality and eye.

I have found some wonderful arts-and-crafts pottery that I don't think I could have afforded to purchase in a regular antique store. Here is why I am telling you about the world through an antique collector's eye. It's not too wet your appetite for more stuff. It's because I'm trying to show you that new doesn't necessarily mean better. Something that was well made in the 1930s remains high quality today. What I look for are not necessarily precious antiques, but unique, beautiful, useful, and inexpensive items. So try it, because I think you are going to like this new mode of shopping. It will completely change your idea of having to shop only in big department stores. Each visit can feel like a mini adventure. Just be careful not to go overboard, like I did!

If We Can Send a Person to the Moon, Why, Fifty Years Later Can't We Make Home Appliances that Last?

I despise the lack of durability our home electronic appliances provide us. Even when you spend more to purchase what you think is a reliable manufacturer's product—with a once–well-thought-of, good old-fashioned manufacturer's name on it—chances are it was not made in this country. Remember all of those manufacturing jobs we lost? Well, those people in other countries are likely making those good old-fashioned products now, and not necessarily as good as or better than we did. I don't know about your house, but at my home we have a vacuum cleaner problem. We have two small dogs, so this is one home appliance we use all of the time. I can't even begin to tell you how many vacuum cleaners we have gone through in the last twelve years. It has to be at least $1,800 worth. Each time the vacuum begins to act up, my husband (who likes dismantling things) tries to revive the blasted thing, and in the end it works for about three months more. But then we have to admit defeat and take the two-year-old vacuum out to the trash bin, where it belonged.

Let me tell you this quick story about the Eureka Mighty Mite. This little orange vacuum cleaner belonged to my mother in the sixties. She always liked it because it was lightweight and she could easily carry it up stairs.

When we had to clean my folks' belongings out of their

home, as we were packing, my husband leaned over to me with his hand on the Mighty Mite and asked, "Does it stay or does it go?" By "go" he meant into the box marked for the Salvation Army. I nodded in the affirmative and then started having second thoughts. In the end, the Mighty Mite came home with us and, believe me, I now know why my mom loved that little orange vacuum cleaner. It has proven itself to be the most reliable home appliance we own. In fact, when our dog, Lily, accidentally knocked over a plant on our new Oriental rug, my husband said while running off, "This looks like a job for the Mighty Mite!" And indeed it was. That vacuum cleaner is quick and never misses a thing. I love that appliance, which was made by the manufacturer fifty or more years ago. I just can't believe it continues working so well and yet we can't find a larger size vacuum cleaner that works as well.

So here is the question: if we could manufacturer an appliance like the Mighty Mite and send a man to the moon in the sixties, why do we proceed to manufacture less-than-acceptable household items fifty years later, which we have to keep replacing?

The same holds true of simple items. Remember when flashlights lasted forever, and all you had to do was change the batteries? Now, it seems when they quit working after a few years, they have to be tossed out. I feel like I always need to buy another $6.95 flashlight. The same could be said for so many home appliances that we don't think twice about having to replace every few years: microwave ovens, toaster ovens, hair dryers, electric toothbrushes, blenders—the list goes on and on. Anyway, I hope it is only in my home that appliances are always frittering out, but I doubt it. I worry that America's home appliances have gone backward in quality, or at least we keep accepting it and keep pulling out the old credit card to replace those items that we had purchased a short time before. If we added it up, we would see that it's a great deal of money we spend every time we have to replace a home appliance that's just a few years old. I find this an unacceptable way to live life. How about you?

Accepting Some Simple Truths

- We have just been through the greatest spending and speculative binge since the 1920s. Our national debt of far over four trillion dollars is a huge tax on our grandchildren that will burden them and future generations for life.
- Our infant mortality rate is the highest in the developed world—twice that of Japan.
- One out of six families in America now is collecting food stamps.
- More than 20 percent of American children are growing up in poverty.
- Our infrastructure is decaying, and our investment in plants and equipment as a percent of GNP now falls below most industrial nations.
- According to Robert Hormats, Under Secretary of State for Economic, Energy and Agricultural Affairs, the story of each generation doing better than the next is perhaps been removed from American

society. He says, " What we are leaving our grandchildren-mountainous debt."

- Informed Americans are all too familiar with the long list of problems now plaguing this country: the explosive issues of poverty and unemployment; the vanishing middle class; the growing group of senior citizens who have lost their pensions, jobs, savings, and investments over the last few years; the high level of crime, violence, and racial conflict; unaffordable and decaying housing; unaffordable health care; rampant political corruption; environmental degradation; a troubled educational system; international crises; and so on.

* * * * * * * * *

Chapter 11
Why Fiscal Discipline Is Like
a Physical Fitness Routine

* * * * * * * * *

*The great and glorious masterpiece of man
is to know how to live to purpose.*
—Michel de Montaigne

Life is full of choices. Abandoning our reckless financial and physical health habits can feel quite drastic at first, as all changes do.

You can decide to work out instead of channel surfing from the couch, or save for a down payment instead of buying designer sunglasses. The same kind of fiscal discipline that applies to living on a budget also rings true for keeping up with a physical fitness regime: Get in your thirty minutes of cardio every day, and contribute the matching amount to your employer-sponsored retirement plan. Put down that doughnut, and save for the future.

Let's be honest. Maintaining our physical and fiscal fitness isn't always the easy—or fun—choice. It requires commitment and stamina, two things that take a lot of energy in an already-busy schedule. Plus, the repetitiveness of staying on track can become quite draining. After a long day at the office, it's a lot easier to park it on the couch and spend twenty bucks on a delivery pizza than to force yourself to pump some iron and go to the market to get healthy ingredients for an inexpensive dinner.

But while it may be tough to stick to a financial or physical fitness plan, the benefits are pretty clear on both counts: gaining financial freedom and good health. For most people, the quality of life is immeasurably better when both your fitness and finances are under control.

If you are right out of college, it isn't easy to pay off college debt when your salary is still quite low. Plus, who as a new graduate did not let your spending habits get a tad bloated? Eventually, though, you need to stop making excuses and start to focus on becoming disciplined and stick to a budget. As the years pass, try to become debt-free. It will feel like a great weight was lifted off your shoulders, and that in itself should make you feel energized.

The same approach to your health and finances works well in tandem. You can begin to learn to view your fitness routine as healthful living, not as a chore. When people first start running, they often feel like their lungs are going to collapse after half a mile, and their muscles burn with each stride. But once they keep at it, they find the benefits really pay off. Their legs get stronger and the exercise becomes cathartic. It takes years of discipline to get to this point, but you can actually begin to look forward to that workout. It leads to a feeling of renewal when you finish your run. Ditto with those food habits.

Sometimes it's hard. It's always a moving target. It's

all about finding balance in finance and fitness. Many of the following twenty items are probably included in your own personal budget. But read closely, because you may be needlessly wasting money. According to *Kiplinger's Personal Finance* magazine, these are some of the issues people needlessly waste their money on. Each item by itself may not seem like it is much money; yet, losing a little here and a little there ultimately results in needlessly wasting money. See if any of these drips (items) are causing you to waste money:

1. **Carrying a balance.** Debt is a shackle that holds you back. For instance, if you have a $1,000 balance on a credit card that charges an 18 percent rate, you blow $180 every year on interest. Get in the habit of paying off your balance in full each month.

2. **Overspending on gas and oil for your car.** There's no need to spring for premium fuel if the manufacturer says regular is just fine. You should also make sure your tires are optimally inflated to get the best gas mileage. And are you still paying for an oil change every 3,000 miles? Many models nowadays can last 5,000 to 7,000 miles between changes, and some even have built-in sensors to tell you when it's time to change the oil. Check your manual to find the best time for your car's routine maintenance.

3. **Keeping unhealthy habits.** Smoking costs a lot more than just what you pay for a pack of cigarettes. It significantly increases the cost of life and health insurance. And you'll pay more

for homeowners and auto insurance. Add in various other expenses, and the true cost of smoking adds up dramatically over a lifetime: $86,000 for a twenty-four-year-old woman over a lifetime and $183,000 for a twenty-four-year-old man over a lifetime, according to *The Price of Smoking*.

Another habit to quit is indoor tanning. There is now a 10 percent tax on indoor tanning services. As with cigarettes, the true cost of tanning, which the World Health Organization lists among the worst-known carcinogens, is higher than just the price you pay each time you go to the salon.

4. **Using a cell phone that doesn't fit properly.** How many people do you know who have spent hundreds of dollars on fancy phones and then pay hundreds of dollars every month for the privilege of using them? Your phone is not a status symbol. It is a way to communicate. Many people pay too much for cell phone contracts and don't use all their minutes. Go to BillShrink.com or Validas.com to evaluate your usage and see if you can find a plan that fits you better. Or consider a prepaid cell phone. Compare rates at MyRatePlan.com.

5. **Buying brand name instead of generic.** From groceries to clothing to prescription drugs, you could save money by choosing the off-brand over the fancy label. And in many cases, you won't sacrifice much in quality. Clever advertising and fancy packaging don't

make brand-name products better than lesser-known brands.

6. **Opening your mouth.** No one wants to be a nuisance. But by simply asking, you may be able to snag a lower rate on your credit card. When shopping, watch for price discrepancies at the cash register, and make a habit of asking, "Do you have a coupon for this?" You might even be able to haggle for a lower price, especially on seasonal or perishable items, floor models, or big-ticket purchases. Many stores will also match or beat their competitors' prices if you speak up. And try asking for a discount if you pay with cash or debit. This saves the store the cut it has to pay the credit card company, so it may be willing to give you a deal. It doesn't hurt to ask.

7. **Buying beverages one at a time.** If you're in the habit of buying bottled water, coffee by the cup, or vending-machine soda, your budget has sprung a leak. Instead, drink tap water or use a water filter. Brew a homemade cup of joe. Buy your soda in bulk, and bring it to work. (Better yet, skip the soda in favor of something healthier.)

8. **Paying for something you can get for free.** There's a boatload of freebies for the taking, if you know where to look. Some of my favorites include credit reports, software programs, prescription drugs, and tech support.

9. **Stashing your money with Uncle Sam rather than in an interest-earning account.**

If you get a tax refund each April, you let the government take too much money in taxes from your paycheck all year long. Get that money back in your pocket this year—and put it to work for you—by adjusting your tax withholding. You can file a new Form W-4 with your employer at any time.

10. **Being disorganized.** It pays to get your financial house in order. Lost bills and receipts, forgotten tax deductions, and clueless spending can cost you hundreds of dollars each year. Start by setting up automatic bill payments online for your monthly bills to eliminate late fees and postage costs. Then get a handful of files to organize important receipts, insurance policies, tax documents, and other statements.

11. **Letting your money wallow in a low-interest account.** You work hard for your money. Shouldn't it work hard for you too? If you're stashing your cash in a traditional savings account earning next to nothing, you're wasting it. Make sure you're getting the best return on your money. Search for the highest yields on CDs and money-market savings accounts.

Your stocks and mutual funds should be working hard for you too. If they've been lagging behind their peers for too long, it could be time to say good-bye. Learn how to spot a wallowing fund or stock.

12. **Paying late fees and missing deadlines.** Return those library books and movie rentals on time. Mail in those rebates. Submit expense reports on time for reimbursement. And if you make a bad purchase, don't just stuff it in the back of the closet and hope it goes away. Get off your duff, return it, and get your money back before you lose the receipt.

13. **Paying ATM fees.** Expect to throw away nearly four dollars every time you use an ATM that isn't in your bank's network. That's because you'll pay an ATM surcharge, and your own bank will hit you with a non-network fee. Consider switching to a bank, such as Ally Bank, that doesn't charge ATM fees and reimburses you for fees other banks charge. Another way to avoid fees is to get cash back when you make a purchase at the grocery store or drugstore.

14. **Shopping at the grocery store without a calculator.** Check how much an item costs per ounce, pound, or other unit of measurement. When you comparison-shop by unit price, you save. For example, if a pack of 40 diapers costs $13, that's 33 cents per diaper. But if you buy a box of 144 diapers for $35, that's 24 cents per diaper. You save 27 percent! (Of course, buying more of something only saves money if you use it all. If you end up throwing much out, you wasted money.)

15. **Paying for things you don't use.** Do you watch all those cable channels? Do you need

those extra features on your phone? Are you getting your money's worth out of your gym membership? Are you taking full advantage of your Netflix, TiVo, and magazine subscriptions? Take a look at what your family actually uses, and then trim accordingly.

16. **Not reading the fine print.** Thought you were being smart by transferring the balance on a high-rate credit card to a low-rate one? Did you read the fine print? Some credit card companies now charge up to 5 percent for balance transfers. Also watch out for free checking accounts that aren't so free. Some banks are starting to charge fees unless you meet certain criteria.

17. **Mismanaging your flexible spending account.** For some people, that means failing to take advantage of their workplace FSA, which lets employees set aside pretax dollars for out-of-pocket medical costs. Other people fail to submit receipts on time. And the average worker leaves eighty-six dollars behind in his or her use-it-or-lose-it FSA account each year, according to WageWorks, an employee benefits provider.

18. **Being an inflexible traveler.** You'll save a lot of money on travel if you're willing to be flexible. Consider traveling before or after peak season, when prices are lower. Or search for flights over a range of dates to find the lowest fare. Booking at the last minute also can save you money because hotels and

airlines slash prices to fill rooms and planes. And flexibility pays off at blind-booking sites, such as Priceline.com or Hotwire.com, which offer deep discounts if you're willing to book a room or flight without knowing which hotel or airline (or other details) you're getting until you pay.

19. **Sticking with the same service plans and the same service providers year after year.** Hey, we're all for loyalty to trusted service providers, such as banks, insurers, credit card companies, mutual funds, phone companies, or cable companies. But over time, as prices and circumstances change, the status quo may not be the best deal anymore. Smart consumers are always on the lookout for bargains.

20. **Making impulse purchases.** When you buy before you think, you don't give yourself time to shop around for the best price. Take the time to compare prices online, read product reviews, and look for coupons when appropriate.

Make it a policy to give yourself a cooling-off period in case you're ever tempted to make an impulse purchase. Go home and sleep on the decision. More often than not, you'll decide you don't need the item after all.

Chapter 12
Cultivating an Everyday Simpler Life

*Enjoy the simple, the natural and the plain.
Along with that comes the ability to do
things spontaneously and have them work.*
—Benjamin Hoff

For many middle-class Americans, the next decade is going to be tough. Adjusting to the new economic realities starts with how you spend your money or, more accurately, how you save your money and learn to get by on less. I am not an alarmist and don't subscribe to scare tactics about America descending into Third World status. That just isn't going to be happening. We're still one of the most prosperous societies in human history, and we're likely to have a decent standard of living for a long time to come. If you want to break it down to raw numbers, economists are projecting that the worst-case scenario is where the average middle-class family might have to adjust to a 20 percent drop in purchasing power. One of the greatest problems currently facing America is that many of us are living with only the bare bones.

Simple Things You Can Do to Save Money

- Make your own morning coffee. I have a little one-cup machine with a steel filter. Why? Because it's easy to operate and clean. I buy really good coffee by the pound, and so a pound of coffee costs $8.50 or so. Buying one large cup of coffee at the coffee shop is approximately $2.50 That means I save money after only four uses, and it doesn't really slow down my getting out the door, especially if I consider how much time it takes waiting in the coffee line.

- On workdays, bring meals from home or find a cheap, repeatable meal. We tend to bleed cash on feeding ourselves, and rarely do we really savor or notice the food. It's just a meal that we consume in between doing other things. The least expensive way is to bring meals from home, and it's also the best way to ensure that you know what you're getting. I'm currently using leftovers or frozen dinners that cost only two dollars a meal, and that's cheaper than any sandwich I can buy. If you have to eat out, try finding the healthiest, best-value meal you can find, and stick to it or slight variations. The more adventurous your meal-seeking gets, the more you will spend.

- Stay out of the pub. Are you in the mood for a few drinks with friends? Bring your own! The cost of a dozen bottles of beer shared among a few friends will always be less expensive than a single drink out at a pub. Surely, one of you has a place to go for the casual entertainment experience, right? Okay, you might not be able to meet attractive members of the opposite sex there, but if your goal is to save on expenses, this is a great way to do it.

- Reconsider your driving habits. Do you have a lead foot? Do you drive around just for something to do? The cost of gas is high, thanks to some interesting "world stage" situations. Pay attention to where you waste gas, and cut down your consumption where possible. It will be money in your pocket. For an added bonus, get out your bike and start to work off that spare tire around your waist!

- If you have an extra room in your house, why not consider renting it? That could help you meet your monthly expenses, especially, if you live anywhere near a college campus where students often want to live outside the dormitories.

- Sum up all your entertainment expenses. When you look at each one separately, it probably doesn't seem weird to pay $8 a month for Netflix, $10 a month for Xbox Live, $60 a month for cable TV, $100 or more a year on various magazines, not to mention all the money you spend when you go to clubs, pubs, bars, concerts, shows, events, coffee with friends, or dinners out. And don't forget those midday snacks. These are all entertainment. If you're working on your debt, tally up all those expenses and look at them as a total sum per month. How much does your entertainment budget really cost, and does that relate to how much money you're putting toward your debts and other expenses? Maybe it's time to reconsider.

- Go on a clothing "fast." You think there are a hundred reasons you need that new shirt or that clever belt. You might need those shoes because they're quite a bargain. But take a good long look at your closet, at what you already have. Do you really need more right now, or should you just start wearing what you already have? How often are you buying clothes for fashion's sake versus need? Can you coordinate new outfits without buying anything new? Have you gone through your accessories lately to see what you have? We buy clothes on impulse more often than just about anything else. Promise yourself not to buy clothes for one month at a time. Say, "I'll go all of August without buying a single article of clothing." At the end of August, assess. Do you really need anything? See if you can go September too.

Fun Ways to Cut Those Nasty Expenses

- **January 1**
  Get free books, music, movies, Wi-Fi, DVDs, and e-books. Have you ever totaled how much money you spend on new books and music in one year? You may be able to go online to place your order for materials, and a librarian will

have them waiting for you when you arrive. You'll find the mother lode of freebies at your public library. All the books, magazines, audio books, video games, and CDs you can carry won't cost a cent. Many libraries also have free Wi-Fi, DVDs, and e-books. And that's not all. Your library may host free book clubs, lectures, film screenings, children's story times, craft activities, and other community events.

- **February 14**

  Delay it, and you'll save a lot of money. If you want to go out and celebrate love on Valentine's Day, just do it a few days before or after the actual date. On Valentine's Day you'll find ridiculously overpriced flowers, and restaurants love to pin you down to an all-inclusive four-course meal for a flat price. If you want to celebrate, there's no need to do it on the fourteenth.

- **March 1**

  Retailers will be getting rid of winter clothing, so buy a new winter coat or boots during this time.

- **April 15**

  Forget that costly gym membership. It doesn't cost a penny to put on a pair of sneakers and go for a walk or jog in your neighborhood. Or check out a workout DVD from your local library. You may also find free instructional workouts in your area. For instance, many athletic stores offer free yoga classes weekly. I also searched the Web and found free tai chi sessions from a variety of organizations in several cities, including San Francisco, Omaha, and New York.

- **May 31**
  Memorial Day usually represents the first weekend when you can pick up some great summertime deals from retailers.

- **June 15**
  If you're a Mac/iPod/iPhone lover, then mark this date down. It's not when Apple will announce new stuff, but it seems like they always announce a new product or updates to existing products in the summer. You'll be able to save on the previous model if you time it right.

- **July 4–September 7**
  Retailers are already starting to unload their outdoors stuff to make way for the fall. August 1 represents the beginning of back-to-school season. You can pick up some great deals on laptops and other consumer electronics.

- **September 1**
  Around Labor Day is when you should start looking to make travel arrangements if you didn't do any traveling over the summer. You

can find the cheapest airline, hotel, and cruise rates during the fall. Just remember, if you vacation in the Southeast or the Caribbean, early fall is peak hurricane season. You may want to consider travel insurance if you purchase during this time.

- **October 1**

  Give yourself an early holiday gift. Get Netflix for $8.99 per month. Going to the movies isn't a great plan if you're trying to save money. But renting movies is easy with Netflix, and there are no late fees.

- **November 1**

  If you're in the market for a new house, start looking in November. Homeowners know that if their house hasn't sold through the fall, there will be fewer shoppers during the winter months, and they are much more likely to ease up on their asking price.

- **December 1**

  Demand from home buyers is low in the winter months, so you'll be able to negotiate with sellers more during these months. You may not be able to get a lot of money reduced on the selling price, but you can negotiate more on mortgage closing costs and extras.

Looking for Unique Ways to Save Money

Saving money on needed purchases is a great way

to … well, save money! Here are some ways to pocket money you might have spent otherwise.

Gift Cards

For the person who has everything (or whose tastes you simply cannot fathom or abide), gift cards are a safe bet. You can find discounted cards at www.giftcardgranny. com. The site pulls prices from six gift card discounters, which buy unwanted cards from other people that they then resell for less than face value. Discounts can be as much as 50 percent, although most are in the 15 to 20 percent range. And the rules for gift cards just became more consumer-friendly.

Closing Costs

If you're buying a house or refinancing a mortgage, you can save by negotiating down the lender's origination fee and other closing costs. Lenders will be willing to strike a bargain for your business if you have great credit and adequate equity. If you're prepared to walk away unless they offer you a great deal, you'll have even more leverage in negotiations.

You might also try hitting up the seller to pay some or all of the closing costs, which average about 3 percent of the purchase price and go as high as 6 percent in higher-tax areas. Freddie Mac and Fannie Mae allow sellers to pick up closing costs worth 6 percent of the purchase price for loans with 10 percent or more down. The Federal Housing Administration allows up to 6 percent (but is considering lowering the limit to 3 percent). And the Department of Veterans Affairs allows 4 percent. You even get a tax break for mortgage points the seller pays (each point is 1 percent of the loan amount).

Checking Accounts

Banks everywhere are eliminating free checking accounts, but with a little creativity you can still avoid paying that extra eight to fifteen dollars a month. If you arrange for direct deposit, maintain a minimum balance, bank online, or skip the paper statement each month, your bank is likely to waive the fee.

About 750 community banks and credit unions offer free checking accounts with no minimum-balance requirement. They'll also pay as much as 3.5 percent interest if you use your debit card ten to fifteen times a month. You can arrange for one automatic payment or direct deposit each month and receive your statement electronically. A partial list is available at www.checkingfinder.com/.

Groceries

The USDA forecasts its 2011 food prices to rise 2 to 3 percent from last year. Dairy prices are expected to be up as much as 5.5 percent, and butter prices have been surging, up 19 percent. This inflation comes at a tricky time for brand-name U.S. food makers, who are seeing consumers shop by purchase cost rather than by well-known manufacturers' names. Most have been reluctant to pass along higher commodity costs. With prices continuing to go up and family incomes stagnating, what's a family to do?

For many families, bulging expenses are a direct result of excess spending at the supermarket. My advice is to ditch the gourmet grocers and even your local large chains you normally shop. Trader Joe's, ALDI, or one of those large warehouse stores can offer you a monthly cost saving. Did you know that Trader Joe's and ALDI are owned by two German brothers? In the 1960s, the two brothers decided to divide up their business, with one brother managing the Trader Joe's operation and the other, Theo Albrecht, who just died, running the ALDI stores. They used their combined bargaining power to lower purchase prices, enabling them to garner higher profit margins while keeping prices low. ALDI is an acronym for "Albrecht Discount." The store's motto is "Concentrating on the basics: a limited selection of goods for daily needs." Trader Joe's states something similar: "Value is a concept we take very seriously. And by value we mean great everyday prices on all of our great products— no sales, no gimmicks, no clubs to join, no special cards to swipe." You have to admire the brothers who brought forth these two different, but similar, types of stores. Trader Joe's carries appeal to shoppers at all income levels. Now, if only all of our grocery stores could be so thoughtful!

Coupons

If you are an organized type of person (which admittedly, I am not), using coupons has never been easier, thanks to the Internet. You can find coupons online, at www.couponmom.com/, www.coupons.com, and www.couponcabin.com/. Or for $5.95 a month, you can get customized coupons from www.shoppingnanny.com. This company will guarantee that if you spend more than $90 a week at the grocery store, you'll save $40 a month using its service—or your next month's membership is free. And of course there always are those incredible deals you can get on Groupon!

Bundling

Bundling your cable TV, phone, and Internet service can save you—dare we say it?—a bundle. For example, you pay just eighty-five dollars a month for twelve months if you sign up online with Verizon for unlimited local and long-distance calling, high-speed Internet service, and DVR service. That saves fifty dollars a month compared with buying the same services separately. This in no way should be interpreted as a recommendation of a specific company's services.

Perhaps one of the best ways to save money is to see if you can live without your cable TV for a month. I don't mean your Internet service also. That would be too much of a hardship for any person to have to endure in this age of Facebook, Skype, etc.

Free Face and Voice Time

E-mail and Facebook are great ways to stay in touch with friends and family, but sometimes you simply need to hear a familiar voice. You might not have free long-distance calling with your phone service. Well, with Skype and Google Talk (you'll need a Gmail account), you can "call" anyone in the United States for free via your computer as long as they have the same software on their computer. If the computers have a built-in camera (webcams cost as little as thirty dollars), you get video as well as audio. Logitech webcam owners can also use the free Logitech Vid service for video calls.

Cell Phone Plans

Wireless carriers keep you tethered to them with two-year contracts and tempt you to renew with snazzy new phones or monthly discounts. But you can slash your costs with a prepaid plan, especially if you're paying extra for text messaging and data plans with your current contract. Also, all of the major carriers, plus a number of smaller firms, offer prepaid plans. Compare them at www.prepaidreviews.com/compare, and then check the carrier's website for more details. Before you compare plans, decide what is most important to you. For example, some providers offer free talk on nights and weekends, no activation or roaming fees, or free 411 calls. I know that all sounds good, but check your past bills to see which costs kept increasing your phone bills every month.

Greeting Cards

We have been listening to that Hallmark marketing slogan, "When you care enough to send the very best," for many years. You can still send the very best, but you don't have to spend three to five dollars to do it. Have you seen the ninety-nine–cent cards at your grocery store? Or you can find hundreds of free cards online that you can send via e-mail. And handmade cards from your children will mean more than a store-bought card. (If you're hosting an event, don't forget about Evites.) If you insist on sending a good old-fashioned card for special occasions, consider packaged cards. The price per card in these packages is very reasonable compared with individual cards. You can buy these packages where you buy all the other individual cards. Buying this way means you will always have a particular type of card on-hand when you need one.

Chapter 13
Brother, Can You Spare a Dime?

* * * * * * * * *

*In helping others, we shall help ourselves,
for whatever good we give out completes the
circle and comes back to us.*
                                    —Flora Edwards

Rather than including the links for all of the following
facts that I found on the Internet, anyone interested
can just Google the particular item of interest and read as
much as they would like. Following are reasons we need
to rediscover the root values of America, our simplicity,
character, and strengths.

#1: We are bleeding middle-class jobs at a staggering
pace. Since 2000, the United States has lost 10 percent
of its middle-class jobs. In 2000 there were about 72
million middle-class jobs in this country; today there are
only about 65 million jobs in that class, with many more
disappearing each month.

#2: The United States is literally hemorrhaging

manufacturing jobs. The decline of manufacturing in America has tremendously accelerated over the past decade. We have lost a staggering 32 percent of our manufacturing jobs since 2000. Back in 1970, 25 percent of all jobs in the United States were manufacturing jobs. Today, only 9 percent of the jobs in the United States are manufacturing jobs. We have literally seen tens of thousands of American factories close down permanently over the past decade. Since 2001, over 42,000 U.S. factories have closed down for good.

#3: Deindustrialization is creating ghost towns in many areas of the United States. Even some of America's biggest cities are now only a shadow of what they used to be. Since 1950, the population of Pittsburgh, Pennsylvania, has declined by more than 50 percent. In Dayton, Ohio, 18.9 percent of all houses now stand empty.

#4: U.S. companies now create more jobs overseas than they do in the United States. Over the past year, American companies have created 1.4 million jobs overseas but less than a million jobs here at home.

#5: When Americans lose their jobs these days, they typically end up having to take new jobs that do not pay nearly as much as their previous jobs. According to one recent study, the majority of unemployed Americans who have been able to find new jobs during this economic downturn have been forced to accept a cut in pay. They have joined the ever-growing ranks of the new "underemployed."

#6: The overwhelming majority of the jobs that the U.S. economy is creating now are low-paying jobs. In fact, more than 40 percent of Americans who actually are employed are now working in service jobs, which are usually very low-paying and often only part-time.

#7: The number of long-term unemployed continues to skyrocket in this country. As 2007 began, there were just over 1 million Americans who had been unemployed for half a year or longer. As of this writing, there are over 6 million Americans who have been unemployed for half a year or longer.

#8: For those who are out of work, the wait can be excruciating. It now takes the average unemployed American over thirty-three weeks to find a job. Many of those will never work again, because many employers brand them as undesirable, with skills rusted due to lack of use.

#9: Millions of Americans have become extremely depressed, discovering that they simply cannot find any work at all. In August 2009, only 10 percent of the unemployed had been out of work for two years or longer. Today that number is up to 35 percent.

#10: The gap between the wealthy and the poor in the United States continues to grow by leaps and bounds. According to one recent report, the wealthiest 1 percent of all U.S. households has an average of approximately $14 million in assets, while the average U.S. household has assets that total about $62,000.

#11: In fact, those at the very top of the income scale seem to be doing better than ever. Between 1950 and 1989, the top 1 percent usually earned around 7 or 8 percent of all national income. Today that figure is getting very close to 20 percent.

#12: Some of the income inequality statistics are almost too outrageous to believe or even think about. For example, the top 20 percent of U.S. working families' take home approximately 47 percent of all income and earn about ten times the amount that low-income working families bring in.

#13: Sadly, most American families are now living week to week. According to a survey released very close to the end of 2010, 55 percent of all Americans are now living paycheck to paycheck.

#14: The U.S. real estate markets continue to stagnate. During the third quarter of 2010, 67 percent of all mortgages in Nevada were "underwater," 49 percent of all mortgages in Arizona were "underwater," and 46 percent of all mortgages in Florida were "underwater." So what happens if home prices go down even more? Don't even ask that question, because things will go up as soon as we get through this rough period. At least, that is my hope. Like many Americans, our home is our retirement money! Just think of what will happen if the real estate market doesn't come back in our lifetime!

#15: For millions of middle-class families, the number-one financial asset has been their house. This does not necessarily have to happen, but unfortunately, many analysts are now projecting that U.S. housing prices will fall much lower than they already have. According to Peter Schiff of Euro Pacific, house prices have to decline at least another 20.3 percent to come back to the historical trend prior to the bubble (www.businessinsider.com/).

#16: Even though home prices have declined significantly, the truth is that they are still too high for most American families. Only the top 5 percent of U.S. households have earned enough additional income to match the rise in housing costs since 1975.

The Middle Class Scrapes Along

#17: Most American families have found that their economic situations have significantly deteriorated over the last several years. In fact, 55 percent of the U.S. labor force since December 2007 have suffered a spell of unemployment, a cut in pay, or a reduction in hours, or they have become involuntary part-time workers.

#18: Tens of millions of Americans barely scrape by; thus, saving for retirement has become impossible for many. Today, 36 percent of Americans say that they don't contribute anything to a retirement account anymore.

#19: The truth is that incomes all across America are going down. In 2009, total wages, median wages, and average wages all declined in the United States. Raises, including cost-of-living raises, are rarer. Just ask my friend who has worked for DuPage County for the past four-plus years. She has received only one cost-of-living raise during that time and one similarly tiny merit raise.

#20: So is anyone doing better? Well, one group is! In 2009, the only group that saw their household incomes increase were those making $180,000 or more.

#21: Most Americans are scratching and clawing and doing whatever they can to make a living these days. Half of all American workers now earn $505 or less per week.

#22: Millions of Americans have been forced to take part-time jobs, because that is all they can get. The number of Americans working part-time jobs "for economic reasons" is now the highest it has been in at least five decades.

USA, USA, USA: Are We Really the Best?

#23: Some of the people who have been hit the hardest by all of this are children. According to one recent study, approximately 21 percent of all children in the United States are living below the poverty line in 2010, the highest rate since the Great Depression.

#24: If all of the above is not bad enough, now our life expectancy has dropped to thirty-sixth place in the world.

Hmm … I think I have the answer to that problem. Could it be that the stress is shortening our lives?

#25: One out of six Americans is on food stamps. (I said this earlier, but I need to say it again because I can't get this out of my head.)

#26: The sad truth is that our country is in decline, and it is getting poorer. Ten years ago, the United States was ranked number one in average wealth per adult. In 2010, the United States has fallen to seventh place.

The Next Balloon to Pop: Student Loan Debt

#26: Our young people are supposed to be the hope for the future, but most of them are up to their eyeballs in student loan debt. Americans now owe more than $875 billion on student loans, which is more than the total amount that Americans owe on their credit cards.

The Life of the Poor Has Gotten Harder!

#27 Life is getting harder and harder for those on the low end of the income scale. The bottom 40 percent of income earners in the United States now collectively own less than 1 percent of the nation's wealth. So are you depressed yet? Well, try not to be. Simply stated, there is a whole lot more to life than just money.

Chapter 14
For Happiness that Lasts, Try This!

Nothing is true, but that which is simple-
—Johann Wolfgang Von Goethe

Have you ever wondered why, with all of our riches, the United States doesn't rank as one of the top countries for having the happiest people? I did, and when I started investigating it I found that when social scientists added the words "happy" and "satisfied with your well-being" to their surveys, the United States actually fell to fifteenth place on that list of happiest societies. These top three may surprise you: (1) Puerto Rico, (2) Mexico, and (3) Denmark. What is it that differs in these societies from the United States? Well, they are "relationship-centric" societies that place a higher priority on family and friends than our culture. Their priorities toward people and relationships result in much greater happiness. It is not "stuff" that results in making people happy, something that Americans are now learning more about.

His Holiness the Dalai Lama says in *The Art of Happiness* that he believes "the purpose of our life is to seek happiness," which most of us would strongly agree with. I love the fact that the price of admission to happiness is the same for everyone—that is, as long as you don't derive your happiness from spending money on extravagant things, which some people do. Make sure that you are inputting the following steps in your life to see if you begin finding more happiness in your everyday life:

1. **Be your authentic self. Don't pretend you are someone you are not.** Human beings all want to be happy at some level. We are almost always on a continuous journey to seek satisfaction. Yet we don't always know where to look, what to do, or even what it would take to make us truly happy. Try to act like the person you want to be, be exactly the person you are, and you will live a comfortable existence.

2. **Your happiness has to start from within.** Happiness can be found in many external things: job success, money, food, cars, alcohol, the opposite sex, etc. People will smile and say that all these things bring pleasure. But the problem with external items is that they are temporary. But internal happiness can last for long periods of time. On your search for happiness, you have to start within. Think of moments when you could say nice things about yourself or had a genuinely good time. What did you do to feel good? Was it the money you earned, or was it that you made your child smile by paying for a pony ride? Was

it the food that you ate, or was it the company you were with who shared the meal with you? Often external objects that bring happiness to us are often extensions of our internal needs. For example, sometimes a young couple will adopt a dog from an animal shelter because they have a need to care for something or someone. Next, along comes a baby!

3. **Look at how you feel toward others.** Once you have received some self-awareness of what makes you happy, take a look at what you do or feel for others that makes them happy. Most people feel some sort of compassion for others and want to do things to help them feel good. We even want to share in others' joy. Think about how people cheer when they see a puppy rescued from being stuck in a pipe or when a cat is rescued from a tree. Many of us have had a pet at one time or another and can feel the pain and, more importantly, joy when someone gets their pet back. When you recognize who or what you feel the most compassion for, you will start to have a sense of direction on what to do to reach that happiness. In fact, if you're feeling impoverished, it is probably time to volunteer at a nearby homeless shelter to give of your time generously. It's a way of showing yourself that you have something to add to someone else's life.

4. **Take confident action, and reach out for that happiness.** Start to do something about

reaching that happiness you felt through compassion. There are countless stories about people who quit their high-paying jobs to pursue simple dreams, just because of the joy they get. Most of those simple dreams involve making other people happy. And don't talk yourself out of it by using negative speak. Saying things like "I'll never be able to" or "I'm not good enough" may lead you right back to those temporary happiness objects ("stuff"). If your happiness comes from food, consider making the meal yourself or making one for a homeless shelter. If you like partying with friends, host a birthday party for a friend. By starting with yourself, reflecting it on others, and taking action, you will be on your way to true happiness.

5. **Focus on what you're grateful for.** Sonja Lyubomirsky, professor of psychology at the University of California, Riverside, and author of *The How of Happiness: A Scientific Approach to Getting the Life You Want*, suggests cultivating a sense of appreciation through something she refers to as a gratitude journal, in which you write down three to five things for which you are thankful. "If you lost your job, think of other dreams that have come true, such as living in the city you want or marrying the right partner. It's not trivializing what's happening, but trying not to focus on it all the time," she says.

6. **Smile. Not only will you feel good, but you will also make someone else feel good.** Perhaps someday in my future I will relate to you some of the medical hurdles I have faced. I really do not want to turn this book into a medical journal of my health woes, because I'm sure many of you have a list of your own. Yet, I want to emphasize one simple truth. Always remember the greatest gift you can give to a complete stranger is a smile. When I smile at someone and that person smiles back at me, I immediately forget my own pain or problems. A simple smile of recognition toward a stranger is a way of communicating that you see that person and that you appreciate sharing the moment, the air you breathe, and the sidewalk on which you walk. You get the idea. Down the street from me is a halfway house filled with people who have varied troubles. When I walk by, rather than trying to avoid making eye contact, I look their way. Sometimes we make eye contact, and sometimes I am rewarded with a smile back—not always, just sometimes. Yet, I see a sense of loneliness amongst these men and women. Just a momentary smile their way I think makes them recognize that they are individuals that society doesn't have to avoid.

Finally, I would only like to add that smiling works very well to help you keep a simpler, uncomplicated life. I don't know why. But I do know it certainly has helped me. I have always remembered this funny moment from years ago. I was sitting in front of the YMCA with my son, waiting for the camp bus to arrive. It was about 7:30 a.m. on this beautiful sunny day. In the distance, I could hear a man's voice singing. At first it was faint, but as he got closer it became louder. Then I was able to make out the words to the song he was singing. It went, "I got plenty of nothin' … and nothin's plenty for me … Folks with plenty of plenty … they've got a lock on the door, while I got plenty of nothin'." This man had plenty of long gray, curly, unruly hair in bad need of a shampoo and brushing. And he was swinging a bag that looked to be an old laundry bag filled with something inside. It could have been all of his clothes. Who knows? As he walked by us, he gave us this sweet huge smile and waved while still singing that song. Seeing this free and happy man on that beautiful morning, with the birds overhead accompanying him, still brings a smile to my face. If you are thinking he was probably some street person, I would say there is a good chance you are right. But his happiness was enviable and simply marvelous, at least in that moment where our paths briefly crossed. The whole image still feels like a priceless gift he gave to me. Thank you, whoever you are!

If achieving happiness is the purpose of our lives, how do we begin to get there? I believe in order to find your unique key to happiness, everyone must begin by understanding themselves and the potential they have. Some people can spend their whole life chasing something they think will make them happy, only to find upon getting where they wanted that it really didn't make them happier. Or perhaps it just wasn't a good fit. It is not always easy finding the happiness key, because it is different for every human being, yet we are all searching for it. That is why we always have to take the time to get in touch and be honest with ourselves, which may be the hardest part.

Here is some interesting info about happiness:

- Money really won't buy happiness. The average household income in the United States more than doubled from about $23,000 to almost $60,000 (adjusted for inflation) from 1950 to 2006, but the level of self-reported happiness remained about the same.

- Happiness is relative. In one study, people preferred a salary of $50,000, as long as they were surrounded by people making $25,000, as opposed to earning $100,000 while others around them made $200,000.

- People who've been through major accidents, even involving paralysis, report the same level of long-term happiness as people who've won the lottery.

It appears, then, that happiness is a state of mind. So how are some people always capable of capturing that state of mind? I decided to do some research on the subject and found that happiness in its simplest form consists of positive emotions and positive activities. Happiness comes to people who create a good life by engaging in activities outside of their normal, day-to-day routines. Research has identified the following correlations with happiness. They are: relationships, social interactions, involvement in a person's community, marital status, employment, health, democratic freedom, optimism, endorphins (released through physical exercise), chocolate (*really!*), religious involvement, the ability to make a good income, and proximity to other happy people. I know for a fact that I love chocolate, and it does make me happy!

Often, the things we believe will make us happy, like having a new car every couple of years or buying the latest fashions, don't really give us a lasting happiness. You cannot look for true, beautiful feelings from material things. In today's world, many people are coming to realize that being caught on the work–spend debt treadmill is not a healthy way to live. Sometimes, people think that to go bigger will make them happier, but it just isn't true and has been proven false many times over. How many times have you seen friends excitedly buy bigger houses for their growing families and find they end up feeling financially strapped and overwhelmed work-wise? They become trapped by all the "stuff" they've hauled into their lives.

"The idea that you need to go bigger to be happy is false," said Ms. Tammy Strobel, who was featured in an August 2010 *New York Times* article about the new "minimalists" in our country. According to Ms. Strobel, "the acquisition of material goods doesn't bring about happiness. It was only upon streamlining my life that I found real happiness."

The recent slowdown in spending by American consumers may actually have an upside. New psychology studies suggest that important to our happiness is having to wait for the anticipated object of interest. The greater the length of time that we have to anticipate and look forward to what we plan to buy, the happier we are about it. The study also shows—and this should be no surprise—there is an increase in happiness when people stop trying to outdo the Joneses. In an economic slowdown it becomes clearly unwise and often impossible to even consider outdoing the Joneses. It's as if we have no choice but to back off on the competition. This eases the pressure on us and simplifies our lives.

"Before credit cards and cell phones enabled consumers to buy anything they wanted, at any time, the experience of shopping was richer," says Ms. Liebmann of WSL Strategic Retail. "You saved for it, you anticipated it," she says. "In other words, waiting for something and working hard to get it made it feel more valuable and more stimulating."

In fact, scholars have found that anticipation immensely increases happiness. Considering buying an iPod? You might want to think about it for as long as possible before taking one home. Likewise about a Caribbean escape. You'll get more pleasure if you book a flight in advance than if you book it at the last minute. So where does the current economic downturn come into play? I really think that our competition for economic displays drives our consumer economy and culture of affluence. In terms of the current mortgage crisis, the findings suggest that one of the reasons we overextend ourselves is that we're basically in a status race. We have expectations that spiral upward as people make more money and everyone wants to show that they are better than average.

Chapter 15
Training for the Revolution: Reversing America's Downward Trend

Lost time is never found again.
—Benjamin Franklin

I found the following information profoundly sad. But I am assuming that most people are thoughtful and intelligent and understand that working to improve our American education is vital to keeping America strong in the future. This area needs everyone's attention more than ever. Now is the time for Americans to strike out on a battle to recommit ourselves to having an excellent American education system that surpasses all others for each and every child. Without this, America stands to lose more than we can even imagine. Our next generations will continue to lose ground on the education pathway, diminishing our abilities to keep up with the technological advances happening all around us.

If you wonder how this ties into living a simple

lifestyle, it's simple. Obtaining a good education, across the globe, means everything to its population. For example, when our country was being established, our forefathers understood the importance of a good education, which is why we have always made education available to everyone and why we built public school systems coast to coast. According to economist Thomas L. Friedman, "America long has been able to attract, develop and unleash creative talent. We have men and women who invent, build and sell more goods and services that make people's lives more productive, healthy, comfortable, secure, and entertained from any other country. And as hard as it is to believe, this may no longer continue."

This comment wouldn't have made sense to me if I hadn't read the Organization for Economic Co-operation and Development (OECD) report two months before. This report illustrates the importance of fixing our schools' problems if Americans intend to stay the strong country it has been. That will not be a simple problem to solve.

According to Friedman, "the only long-term solution to America's problems has to be growing our way out of debt with American workers who are more empowered and educated to compete. We need to use our now diminishing resources in the most efficient way possible to get back to our core competency, which will require our American youth to be well-educated to remain competitive with other nations across the globe."

In the December 27, 2010, issue of *Newsweek* magazine, billionaire philanthropist Bill Gates and president of the American Federation of Teachers Randi Weingarten were interviewed with the hope of finding common ground to fix our nation's education system. Bill Gates, responding to a question regarding America's education status in the world, said, "Well, it's the big issue. A lot of other countries have put effort into their school systems. So part of it is the competition is better. The Chinese, who have a 10th of our wealth, are running a great education system. There are some things we can learn from other systems. They have a longer school day in most countries and a longer school year in most countries. And some of them have elements of their personnel system that are worth learning from."

Were you aware that the number of U.S. high school graduates ranks near the bottom among developed nations? And on virtually every international assessment of academic proficiency, American secondary school student performance varies from mediocre to poor. Given that human capital is a prerequisite for success in the global economy, U.S. economic competitiveness is looking unsustainable, with poorly prepared students feeding into the workforce.

In the job market of the future, rivals will be well-educated students from Sydney, Hong Kong, and Singapore, competing for the same jobs. So, while globalization has progressed, our American educational progress has stagnated, according to the OECD report. Amazingly, American universities are still considered to be the best in the world and continue to attract students from every continent. I just wish we had more American students who could still get into some of our top universities.

This information is showing us that, since the 1980s,

the modern workplace has radically changed, yet our workforce is not adequately being prepared for the new job requirements. To round off this intimidating news, the rapidly growing minority populations that represent a disproportionate share of America's lowest-achieving students are projected to make up more than half of the U.S. population by 2050 (United States Census Bureau 2004). Unless the United States begins to prepare all students for college and the modern workplace, America's disturbing downward trend is only going to get worse.

While I was in the midst of preparing the manuscript for *A Simplicity Revolution*, I was pleased to be able to see the excellent documentary film "Looking for Superman," which illustrates our broken education system in America and how injurious it is to our culture and our global future. I highly recommend your viewing it when it becomes available to you.

International surveys now show America's performance gap between the highest and least proficient students just continues to grow. This wide gap is amongst the highest of all countries. In the United States, one-quarter of U.S. fifteen-year-olds do not reach the baseline level of science achievement. This is the level at which students begin to demonstrate the science competencies that will enable them to use science and technology in life situations. And just in case that hasn't convinced you of the sorry state our American educational system, according to the Organization for Economic Co-Operation, our fifteen-year-olds ranked seventeenth in science and twenty-fifth in math skills. We now rank twelfth among developed countries in college graduation, which is down from number one for decades.

In 2010, the annual in-state cost for the typical state university soared to more than $15,000, and private colleges now charge an average of $35,600 a year. In the past, American college graduates could expect to land a nice job following their graduation and quickly begin paying off their student loans. But then the Great Recession put many jobs out of reach for new college graduates, who, unlike some of the generations before them, are going to begin their lives in debt. So the American future is looking different now for new college graduates, because they are the first generation to be carrying so much student debt. What could be better than being a young smart man or woman, a recent college grad, starting out life, and looking to find a job, an apartment, and possibly even a used car to get to work? But on top of these expenses, you will have one more bill for the next decade: your monthly college repayment expense. Yes, America's youth, we know you can do it!

Perhaps some of my outrage about the high cost of a college education these days is because we are trying to help pay for my son's college. But I have come to the conclusion that the outrageous cost of a college education in America is out of control. Long-term price trends make higher education an especially inflationary sector of the U.S. economy, with tuition increases in recent years sometimes outpacing even the explosive health-care sector. These trends are the sources of continuing controversy in the United States, because the cost of higher education is just making the great American dream even harder to obtain. Where has the fairness and social justice in our education system gone? Could the American university system be the next bubble to burst in America? Will we have students protesting at American universities, like we saw students doing in England and Italy under the slogan "They are blocking our future"?

This is a call to action for all Americans, to personally and publicly take the time to invest in America's failing education system. If we wish to see America continue to be known as a world leader, we certainly will need to fix this problem.

We can rise to our "better selves"!

* * * * * * * * *

Chapter 16
Technology and Relationships

* * * * * * * * *

Progress is man's ability to complicate simplicity.

—Anonymous

Here we are in the twenty-first century, well-known for its digital technology strides, yet so many of us feel like we have less time than ever to decompress, unwind, relax. During the early stages of its mainstream use in the 1980s and 1990s, digital technology became widely accepted by most of the world. Common business practices (such as tracking different accounts and personal information), schoolwork (researching information for anything and everything), and home life (paying bills and tracking expenses) became simpler, and it all was due to the digital age in which we live. Young people growing up during these massive technological changes are known as the "digital natives," a term that needs little explanation. Having grown up with so many different technologies, these people are extremely comfortable multitasking, using several different technologies at one time. The research is still not complete on how well this multitasking actually serves a person and will probably be analyzed by all kinds of researchers over the course of the upcoming years. We still are waiting to learn how the human brain can cope with these new technologies.

But if anyone is questioning the social connections (relationships) that this new age technology has created for us, one only needs to look at how much of an impact Facebook has had on our world. Who would have predicted that Facebook would enable this generation of youth to engage in peaceful revolutions in the Middle East or places where political freedom was not tolerated, like Tunisia and Egypt, where dictators had been firmly entrenched for over thirty years? There are also regular uprisings in countries in North Africa. The following countries are teetering closer to becoming democratic every day: Jordan, Yemen, Bahrain, Libya, and Iran. I still have to pinch myself to know I'm not dreaming. I'm sure the young people who invented Facebook and Twitter never had this in mind when it was first being created. To think that this societal software program was able to enable like-minded people to face-down their dictators in Tunisia and Egypt, is really quite incredible. I believe it is only going to be a matter of time before all political leaders wake up to the fact that technologies have created a door for democracy to enter. Facebook, which spread like a fast-moving spring rainstorm on the move, has now penetrated throughout the world, getting into places where no outside media was once tolerated. It has enabled us to see and hear things that previously nobody in the outside world was allowed to. And, like I said earlier, who would have thought that this simple tool could change the world for this new generation of men and women? Archaic and despotic governments need to understand that the youth of our world have seen democracies in action and, apparently, they like what they see! China, I do hope you are learning from this!

When online social networks exploded onto the scene, Facebook proved the winner of the pack. And for older generations who desperately tried to resist joining, eventually they caved from the pressure from friends and family members, and they joined too. A friend of mine told me how her grown son called her "antisocial" because she didn't like Facebook. The pressure to join is heavy! Rather quickly, people all over the world were Facebooking it, and once again, another American technological invention went viral.

This digital world is changing the direction of so many lives in ways that could not have been foreseen even one year ago! For example, long-lost friends and family members have been able to reconnect, and that's a good thing. People with similar interests are able to find each other and talk about their passions. And, of course, it didn't take long for companies and politicians to see the immense marketing benefits that Facebook had to offer them, did it?

In his book *Ethics for the New Millennium*, the Dalai Lama says, "Sometimes we become so caught up with the idea of acquiring still more and better stuff that we make no room for anything else in our lives. Yet, all we really want is a connection with each other. In today's world, we tend to rely on machines for our connections. In fact, modern living is organized in such a way that it demands the least possible direct dependence on others, therefore leading to more feelings of loneliness and alienation."

I sometimes have found technology to be very invasive in our family life, and friends have often told me that I am not alone in these feelings. As hard as I have tried to preserve the old-fashioned dinnertime in our home, I know that I have not been successful. My husband, who owns his own small software company, is often on the road, visiting clients. Sometimes he will be gone two weeks out of the month. Even when he is in town, he is working in his home office, and he works there from 7:30 a.m. to 7:00 p.m. So although we work out of the same home, we don't see much of each other.

This has made it hard for our whole family to sit down together to eat dinner. I have always regretted not being able to offer my son the same sense of tradition that I grew up with, which was a reliable family meal every night. Of course, our times have certainly changed, and probably not too many families can sit down for a family meal together every night. But how I miss those simpler times!

When I was a kid, my mom would reliably begin cooking around 4:30 p.m., and my father was always home around 5:30 p.m. My parents, my sister, and I would sit down to eat by 6:00 p.m. We would either talk or fight, but the nice thing was that we were all together and could count on it.

Although nobody could argue that computers serve to simplify our lives, they have also brought about a new addiction, according to health professionals. There are now growing concerns about stress and a rise of antisocial behavior from the overuse of mobile phones, the Internet, and related technologies. The term "Internet addiction disorder" is used when someone's personal daily life is being interfered. In the future, this may be classified as a psychological disorder. Some of the online activities that normally would be considered troublesome are compulsive game playing, gambling, or shopping. These are also referred to as net compulsions. And here is something that's interesting to me: not only are our kids and teenagers playing these computer games, but grownups are playing in an addicted fashion, as well.

Are there any parents out there who haven't tried to coax their kid off the computer by using something they thought would surely work, only to realize that those dang games win every time?

In the past, a wife would often complain that her husband spent too much time on weekends in front of the TV, watching sports all day long. Today, it is not unusual to read stories about wives or husbands complaining about their spouse's addiction to the Internet. In some cases, this addiction leads to actually breaking up marriages when, for example, a spouse learns his or her partner has been "hooking up" with somebody from the Internet. That looking-up of old girlfriends/boyfriends, or somebody new, can lead a troubled marriage to either counseling or splitting up.

Here is another downside from all of this technology. Adults working with teens in recent years say they are seeing an unsettling strain of desensitivity among young people. In May, University of Michigan's Institute for

Social Research issued a report on an analysis of 72 studies on the empathy of nearly 14,000 college students between 1979 and 2009. The result was that today's college students are about 40 percent lower in empathy than students two or three decades earlier. The researchers suggested that disheartening trend may have to do with numbness created by violent video games, an abundance of online friends, and an intensely competitive emphasis on success, among other factors.

Concerned about what he perceived as growing desensitivity, Jay Kyp-Johnson, psychologist at Prospect High School in Mount Prospect, Illinois, decided to confront it early in the school year at a meeting of the student leadership group, Knights' Way, by asking a simple question: "Is it popular to be mean?" And, to an overwhelming degree, Kyp-Johnson recalled they said, "Yeah, it is sort of popular to be mean." He and others said that "desensitivity may start with the impersonal nature of technology in the hands of impulsive, immature people ill-equipped to think through the consequences of what they say—or text, or post on Facebook."

"Previous generations typically were forced to speak directly to someone, even if it was on the phone, or perhaps write a note or letter to the person they had an issue with," Kyp-Johnson said. "With texting and social networks, it's all at your fingertips and it's instantaneous." And with a couple of keystrokes, venomous attacks can spread to thousands of people. That environment, along with the glib, harsh language that has become the norm on TV shows (especially reality TV) and coarse content all over the Internet, has popularized desensitivity.

As this above example shows, not all creative digital advances have necessarily been good for our society. There is no question that our digital advances around the world have been beneficial. The Internet will be a key component of simple living in the future. We are already shopping online more and more, thus reducing the use of our cars. Also, by working from home we are now reducing our carbon footprint with telecommuting, and we are less reliant on paper. Simple living may include high-tech components (like computers and the Internet), wind and water turbines, as well as a variety of other cutting-edge technologies within our mainstream culture.

MIT professor Sherry Turkle questions in her new book, *Alone Together*, "Yet, with all of this use of technology, doesn't that give us all the more reason to keep simplicity in sight and work to maintain our humanistic views of the real world? Do people really feel more connected because they use Facebook?" This book is a fascinating portrait of our changing relationship with technology and the result of nearly fifteen years of study (and interviews with hundreds of subjects). Turkle writes, "Technology has redefined our perceptions of intimacy and solitude—and warns of the perils of embracing such pseudo-techno relationships in place of lasting emotional connections."

Unlike Sims City, the computer game that allows you to manage life in your own city, or Farmville, which allows you to manage your life on the farm, this is no computer game we are living in. No, our everyday lives are real. And people, especially kids and teens, need to keep in touch with reality in ways other than by computers and social networking. For example, when I am talking to someone I feel comfortable with, I usually touch that person's arm or shoulder as I'm talking, which psychologists would probably say is a display of warmth toward the person. When I am talking with friends on the Internet, we exchange jokes and information, but it's just not the same. I want to feel my friend's presence and hear her laugh out loud instead of reading those "LOL" or "Haaaaaaaaaaaaaaaaaa" messages. Don't get me wrong, I am a big fan of the social network technology, but I don't think Facebook is a substitute for real community (i.e., neighborhoods). It may represent one, but it isn't yet. In this drama called life, we have to remember to spend real face time with family and friends and not rely on screen time as a substitute. That goes for Skype as well, because although it may seem the same, it's not.

While out at a restaurant for dinner, I see parents wrestling with the same technology issue my family faced, which is their son or daughter listening to an iPod rather than joining in the family conversation. I can also remember looking over at my son, who would be checking his e-mail every second. My husband and I would be hearing the annoying noise his iPhone makes each time an e-mail comes. You would think he was running IBM or something like that. And here was the real kicker. He would constantly want to e-mail right back. I would calmly say to him (and sometimes not so calmly), "Put that away now, please. What could be so urgent that you need to reply during dinner to an e-mail?" Keep it simple: no smartphones in restaurants or at home during mealtime. It will eliminate arguments that parents don't need during dinnertime, and it will keep your time together free of distractions from the outside world.

If you are a Skype user, you will appreciate this story. Some families use Skype or their cell phones to talk with family members even within the same house but on a different floor. I know this because, sadly, it happens all the time in my house. Also, my son was getting ready to leave for college, and I was warned at the university parent/student orientation to not expect your kids to be calling home much, because they prefer text messaging home. When I heard that I thought, *That stinks!* I wanted to hear my kid's voice! But although I hated text messaging, I was willing to become the best text messenger in the world if that was what it would take to stay in contact with my son. Then one day my son, now a freshman in college, Skyped me, and what a gift that was! If you are not familiar with Skype, you should be. All you need to do is download the software onto your computer and/or phone, have a webcam placed on your computer, and for free not only can you talk to people in almost any country, but you will see them live, as if they are in the room talking to you. I couldn't believe it. Why had I not thought of that before he left for college? We now regularly Skype each other and keep up on each other's news, which is a parent's dream. What could be better? In fact, I said to my son via Skype yesterday that it dawned on me that we were getting to see and talk with each other more now that he's away at college than we did his whole last year of living at home. We both started laughing at that because we knew it was true. Skype is allowing us to get back to that wonderful face-to-face visiting that was falling by the wayside with cell phones and text messaging. It's simplifying our lives by bringing us back to face-to-face communication. Believe me, this is not a paid advertisement for Skype! I'm just a very content consumer in this case.

Chapter 17
Shape up, America!

You are never too old to set another goal or to dream a new dream.

—C. S. Lewis

Not only can our government do a better job, but our corporate executives, the nonprofit world, and our citizenry in general can, as well. It's character-building time, folks. As a people, we have done far less than our best. We have proven in earlier crises that we are better than what we have shown our next generation and, in fact, the world over this past decade. We need to prove ourselves once again.

We have just been through the greatest spending and speculative binge since the 1920s. Our national debt is far over $4 trillion and will, in effect, be a burdensome tax on our grandchildren. Speaking of taxes, shouldn't the tax break that was granted to the very rich under President Bush be abolished once and for all? The way I see it, anyone who speaks against the trillion-dollar–deficit situation that this country is in, yet lobbies to keep this tax break that originally was supposed to be temporary for the top 1 percent earners in America so that they could create more jobs for the economy—well, I think they are nothing more than hypocrites. Here's why. In August 2010, the Congressional Budget Office (CBO) estimated that extending the tax cuts for the 2011–2020 time period would add $3.3 trillion to the national debt, comprising $2.65 trillion in foregone tax revenue plus another $0.66 trillion for interest and debt service costs. *Ouch!* The nonpartisan Pew Charitable Trusts estimated in May 2010 that extending some or all of the tax cuts would have the following effect under these scenarios:

- Making the tax cuts permanent for all taxpayers, regardless of income, would increase the national debt $3.3 trillion over the next ten years.
- Limiting the extension to individuals making less than $200,000 and married couples earning less than $250,000 would increase the debt about $2.2 trillion in the next decade.
- Extending the tax cuts for all taxpayers for only two years would cost $561 billion over the next ten years.

Here is where good old-fashioned ethics are revealed. If anyone can look me in the eye and explain how they can argue this issue out of both sides of their mouth, please start right now, because I have never heard a convincing argument!

Our infant mortality rate is the highest in the developed world—twice that of Japan. More than 20 percent of American children are growing up in poverty. What we're leaving our grandchildren is mountainous debt. Our infrastructure is decaying and our investment in plant and equipment as a percentage of GNP falls below most industrial nations. Informed Americans are all too familiar with the list of problems: the explosive issues of poverty and unemployment, crime and violence, racial conflict, housing, health care, political corruption, and so on, not to mention our environmental degradation and our troubled educational system.

My favorite commentator, Mark Shields, noted in his syndicated column last fall,

> *An America without optimism is an America lacking confidence either in his or her future. For the country's as well as the world's well-being, Americans—who include the leaders and all us followers— must determine to recapture that native optimism and the national sense of confidence it inspires. Unless we can, we risk dooming our own children's futures. Confidence and trust will continue to be tested. Yet, if we draw on our indigenous dynamism and constructively figure out what it takes to create a can-do future more faithful to our history, then maybe all those ruminations about decline and fall could be warnings without warrant. In other words, it's up to all of us.*

I applaud Mr. Shield's very well-stated call for all citizens to shape up!

In my humble opinion, one of our biggest challenges

for the future will come in confronting the political polarization and dysfunctions we have been seeing happen head-on. It is this hurdle I am concerned about that is currently testing our democracy. A friend and I were talking about our political polarization, and we were trying to figure out how things got so bad. I traced it back to 1991, when President Bill Clinton got elected. Do you remember that Whitewater investigation, headed by Kenneth Starr? Ever since that time, the Republicans and the Democrats have fought. Whatever happened to passing legislation that is in the best interest of "We the People"? We can no longer allow our problems to stagnate. Today in America, we need shoulder-to-the-wheel solutions and lawmakers who understand that decision making cannot be formulated regarding how it will affect their next election. Some solutions to problems cannot hang on those types of matters.

I like to think that for everything that happens there is a reason. It simplifies things for me to be able to look at a negative situation and ask, "What is the reason for this?" That sort of personal interrogation allows some truths to float to the surface, which helps me to sort out what has happened and why. I see this time in America as our need for a cleansing of sorts. Maybe we needed to be reminded, enlightened, that a culture of "buy this" and "buy that" is too complex to be healthy, especially when we are always pulling out our credit cards to make those purchases that we are pretending we can afford, when in reality we can't.

Urban theorist Richard Florida's article, "How the Crash Will Reshape America," published in the March

2009 issue of *The Atlantic*, takes an extensive view of the Great Recession that caused America's crash. The best word to describe what he sees happening in America is "reshaping." At the end of his article's introductory paragraphs, he predicts that "recession and decline will spread outward from New York to Detroit and the Sun Belt in a way that will permanently alter, or reshape, America's economic landscape." In a sort of apocalyptic fashion, he writes, "It will permanently and profoundly alter the country's economic landscape. I believe it marks the end of a chapter of American economic history, and indeed, the end of a whole way of life."

I agree with Mr. Florida that there are going to be prolonged and extensive changes coming to America. I also believe the results will ultimately be beneficial. It reminds me of an old Chinese proverb: "When the winds of change blow, some build shields against the wind. But others build wind mills." Or this old American saying: "When life gives you lemons, make lemonade!"

America Faces Toughest Time Since World War II

Change can be great, or it can be awful. I prefer to take an optimistic view and look at how we can work the change to our favor. What's important is our reaction to change. We may not be able to control the change, but we can surely control our reaction. For someone who has just lost a job that she's been doing for the last eighteen years, the prospect of finding a new job during these times is daunting, even terrifying. Today's trying times may require people to learn some new and different skills to make them more employable. Even then people will wonder if the training will pay off and help them land a new position. The key is to stay humble and give yourself time to learn. Learning something new in life can actually be fun and challenging. Allow yourself room to make some mistakes, without being too hard on yourself.

The telltale signs over the past ten years that something unusual was happening in our economy became more and more noticeable. Everyone's response to the bleak economic headlines was "Oh my gosh" or worse. Remember the Y2K scare at the beginning of this century? Well, the rest of the decade's news didn't go so well either:

Obama Raises 2010 Deficit Estimate to $1.5 Trillion

Bloody Monday: 74,000 Layoffs Announced in One Day

Bank Failures, Bank Closings, FDIC Receivership

Citigroup Bank May End Up With U.S. Bailout

The North American Auto Industry in Crisis

And just when we thought it couldn't get any worse,

Report: 9,000 Jobs Leave California Each Year

Mortgage Crisis Surpasses Other U.S. Debt Crisis

!! Holy_*#@

We were hit by a tsunami of bad news—not just once,

but day after day, week after week, month after month. People are nervous after seeing family members or friends losing their jobs, along with their pride. We had to watch home values sink; our 401(k)s are going down, while income and property taxes continue to climb. In fact, Americans are losing jobs at a rate unseen in this century, and that includes the Great Depression. Additionally, those currently trying to find replacement jobs in the workplace are being challenged to find any job, even a part-time job, for survival.

Ageism in the job market prevails, in good times and bad, and it is very difficult to get excited about starting a new job when you have been in the trenches for thirty years. So, if your 401(k) is gone, your job is gone, you cannot survive on your Social Security, and you are being forced into an early retirement that you cannot afford, if you are lucky, perhaps we'll be seeing you at a Walmart store, when you greet us.

At times, it feels like we have been sliding downhill into a world of poverty, hunger, wars, and violence. I believe, however, that America, like so many other times before, will eventually regain its stride. We have a culture that stresses entrepreneurship, positive thinking, and taking time to care about ourselves, our families, our communities, and our planet.

It seems like ages ago that Americans came to expect luxury and entitlement based on decades of endless economic growth and power. The changes we've experienced have felt so radical over the last few years. Today the average citizen is facing economic uncertainty and the prospect of hardship. Did we really think our consumer euphoria could continue without a significant change? Yes, we did. But now it's time to look at what will simplify this picture and figure out how to make do with less.

Returning to a simpler America does not mean turning our backs on the technological world that we have helped to create. No, it means embracing an unpretentious, down-to-earth lifestyle with the knowledge that we don't need to live a life of luxury to live a life of happiness and contentment.

Living with more technological advances than any generation before ours is enriching us in many ways, yet it has consequences that most of us are not prepared for. Our lives are now more complex. We are challenged constantly to upgrade our knowledge, be in touch with more people than ever, and constantly improve our technological base. We are busy, hurrying to our next task with little time for reflection. Many of our kids have schedules as busy as Fortune 500 executives. The sad thing about this is that, by having such hectic schedules, we don't have time to enjoy and reflect on why we do the things we do! This makes our need for simplicity all the more crucial, because without it we can lose our sense of true purpose.

Because I really like birds, I like looking at our lives, as if we are all trying to catch a beautiful bird. Like birds, our lives are beautiful. Still, each moment is so hard to seize, akin to that beautiful bird. I use the word "seize" only because that is the imagery I like to use in my own life. I have always loved the phrase "carpe diem," which is Latin for "seize the day." It is a phrase from a poem by Horace and means "to enjoy, seize, and make use of." I adore this phrase, because it reminds me how each moment of my life is precious and not to sweat the inconsequential things in life.

Since we are living in a time of such great change with joblessness at record highs, I hope you can still see that you can afford to live the life that you dream of by living smarter and embracing simplicity, which is what a Simplicity Revolution is all about. I hope you'll be inspired to reflect on the next steps you are going to take to living a fuller, satisfying, and simpler lifestyle.

Have we allowed how we dress or the car we drive to "brand" us, or identify how successful we are? Sometimes, it's the people who can afford anything they want who are the most miserable. That's because they have no time or don't take the time for self-reflection and examining more closely the world around them. In his sonnet, "The World Is Too Much With Us," William Wordsworth wrote, "The world is too much with us—getting and spending, we lay waste our power ..." Just think how relevant that verse is to what we all just witnessed in the last decade!

Chapter 18
Looking to a Simplicity
Revolution for Answers

When from our better selves we have too long been parted by the hurrying world, and droop. Sick of its business, of its pleasures tired, how gracious, how benign in solitude.

—William Wordsworth

Simplicity and solitude are crucial to collecting a person's thoughts and rediscovering our "better selves" away from the hurrying world around us. Did you know that people are intuitively attracted to simplicity? Probably because if this is the lens from which you view life, you are able to clearly see the commercial manipulation and deceit around you every day.

From the time we get up in the morning until we go to bed at night, we have stressors all around us: the

Great Recession, home foreclosures, job losses, unending technological changes, climate change, wars in Iraq and Afghanistan, news about Iran and North Korea, etc.

The way I see it, only when we simplify (i.e., find our focus, stop running in circles, get on a definable path, and keep every form of clutter at bay) can we hope to be our best selves. It is that which can make a tight-knit, high-functioning home, community, society, nation, and world. Worst selves lead to chaos and confusion, the downward spiral in which we find many facets of our society today.

Corporations made up of best selves will provide jobs right here in America, pay living wages to American workers, train today's workforce to work in the competitive jobs of tomorrow, and budge a bit on the bottom line in order to avoid layoffs. Best selves in homeownership will pay attention to the tiny print when signing mortgage loan documents and will sincerely assess whether they can afford to get into such an arrangement. Best selves in the banking industry will keep the customer in mind and clearly explain the tiny print. Best selves in the world of technology will work to make systems truly user-friendly and reliable, recognizing, for example, that an aging population finds it harder to keep up with all the changes, if only on a financial level and possibly even at a technical level. When it comes to the issue of climate change, we need everyone to be their best selves. Then we must pass on to our kids those values that we hold regarding consumption and recycling. We will pass on the same to our neighbors and our government representatives. Our best selves will simplify our lifestyles, focusing on what is important in the long run and thinking twice (or more) when tempted to accumulate stuff. When our best selves keep homes that focus on family and friends rather than on furnishings, for example, just think of how much simpler our lives will be.

Have you ever done any home remodeling? Remember the chaos of workers coming in and out of the house all day, the hammering, the drilling, the scraping, the chemical smells? How many times did you tell yourself, "I'll never do this again"? Remember the stress levels? Did you really have to have that work done? Did you really have to add that expense to your life? Now think about how things would have been different had you settled for the way things were before the remodeling. Would you have survived? Would you have had more time for family and had a healthier environment in your home that didn't involve stretching your budget beyond your comfort zone? The next time you think of complicating your life, think again. This goes far beyond home renovations. Making the opposite, simpler choice might leave more time for everyone in the family to be their best selves, because there will be fewer distractions and more money in the bank.

The same can be said of the challenges America faces boosting our education system. Better selves work toward an answer to the problems that have arisen over the last few decades, just as we need our best selves to work on bettering government relations and instilling more harmony into our system of government. Worst selves would just go on complaining about problems without working to find solutions. Also, our better selves don't just look for those simple answers. We insist on using logic and truth to make important decisions.

Let us hope that America's better selves will be able to confront America's future political polarization and dysfunction head-on. This will test the country's capacity for adaptable self-correction and involve a collective decision that we will no longer allow our problems to stagnate. Our better selves' shoulders-to-the wheel solutions seem to be imperative.

During what is, for many people, still a troubling time, I hope that I have left you with some beneficial things to think about in the midst of your daily life. As the Dalai Lama says, "If there is a solution, what is the point in being anxious? Be content to apply it. And if there is no solution, what is the point in being anxious? Anxiety will only make your suffering worse."

It is time for us to move forward. Our economy will eventually recover from this downturn, and with it the same opportunities and problems shall return. If anything good has come out of these trying times, perhaps it is that a life of abundance does not have to relate to how much "stuff" we have, but rather the relationships that are in our lives.

Simplicity in life eases my mind every time!

In Closing

Having read many different books about religion and economics, I would like to introduce a Buddhist way of thinking about America's Great Recession, which I have found beneficial. They say the mind is the creator of the world and our universe has different cycles. Thus, going forward in life, I hope you can take hold of that concept. It is you, your mind, creating the type of world that you want to live in. So although this Great Recession may begin to feel like it is going on forever, in the overall scheme of life, it is no more than a blink of the eye. History has taught us that this nation's pendulum has a way of always righting itself to the middle. In fact, America's best days may still lie ahead. So keep the faith, and always remember that simplicity is freedom!

Addendum
Simplicity Through the Ages

More than 2,400 years ago, founders of western philosophy found "simplicity" as a characteristic to be greatly valuable because it revealed an understanding of life itself. It put value on reflective thoughts more than things. Don't you find it amazing that people living in the fourth century BCE were thinking about simplicity in such a significant manner? It is intriguing to think that the great philosophers were writing profoundly about simplicity in 352 BCE. What could have possibly been so difficult or stressful? Perhaps simplicity is just a human desire that all of mankind has always shared. We all think we are overburdened and need to slow down, to simplify, and to give quietness a chance. To Socrates and Plato and other great philosophers, simplicity meant taking time to examine and value life itself and finding the quiet center of one's soul. Isn't it amazing how this demonstrates that people throughout the ages have wrestled with the same issues we continue to wrestle with today?

Simplicity is sometimes elusive, but it is almost always available to us. Sometimes we just need to know where or how or that we should look for it. Luckily, many perceptive thinkers over the years have made it a point to share their thoughts on simplicity in the form of quotes and proverbs that we can borrow and build on. When you look back and see what some of the founders of western philosophy say about simplicity: it truly is exciting and inspiring.

The ancient Greek philosopher, Socrates, came up with the following steps to building a life, which he describes as "a good life is a life worth living." He taught this four-step formula, which still resonates as a way to live one's life:

1. Be. The nearest way to glory is to strive to be what you wish to be thought of. Be as you wish to seem. (It sounds like the modern expression, "Fake it 'til you make it.")

2. Know. Know yourself. The unexamined life is not worth living.

3. Know your limitations. I know that I am intelligent, because I know that I know nothing.

According to Socrates, only the wisest of people are fully aware of their limitations. Saying to someone "I don't know, but I'll find out" is a great thing to say! Try it more often, and you'll be surprised how much better your life will be. Then, just know more.

Nature has given us two ears, two eyes, and but one tongue—so that we should hear and see more than we speak. Expand your horizon, start to observe more, and it helps you grow mentally. "Education is the kindling of a flame, not the filling of a vessel," Socrates said. Always remember to have a meaning to your education, to help you illuminate your life and guide your way, not just to fill a vessel.

4. Improve yourself inside out. He who is not content with what he has would not be content with what he would like to have.

Once you have gone through all four steps of Socrates' formula for a good life worth living, hopefully you will begin feeling more mindful of the importance of simplicity as a life path to happiness.

Next, the Greek philosopher, Diogenes, in 323 BC maintained that all the artificial growth of society was incompatible with happiness and that morality implies a return to the simplicity of nature. He said, "It is simplicity that makes the uneducated more effective than the educated when addressing popular audiences." You really have to admire this ancient man, who already was witnessing a growth of an element of artificiality in society, which he proclaims is incompatible with happiness. It is amazing that, centuries ago, this man could see the danger of modernity, those "fancy talker" types who were already creeping up on the ancient Greeks. Then, we have the ancient Greek philosopher, Plato, who is thought to be a student of Socrates. He is the world's most influential philosopher and lived in 428 BC. Plato said, "Wise men speak because they have something to say; fools because they have to say something." Plato is also famous for saying, "The unexamined life is not worth living."

Literary and Historical Quotes

Leonardo da Vinci (1452–1519): Renaissance painter, scientist, and thinker. *Simplicity is the ultimate sophistication.*

Confucius (551 BC–479 BC): Chinese philosopher. *Life is really simple, but men insist on making it complicated.*

Henry Wadsworth Longfellow (1807–1882): U.S. poet. *Simplicity in character, in manners, in style; in all things the supreme excellence is simplicity.*

Ralph Waldo Emerson (1803–1882): U.S. poet, essayist, and lecturer. *It is proof of high culture to say the greatest matters in the simplest way. Nothing is simpler than greatness; indeed, to be simple is to be great.*

Frédéric Chopin (1810–1849): Composer, virtuoso pianist, and music teacher. *Simplicity is the final achievement. After one has played a vast quantity of notes and it is simplicity that emerges as the crowning glory.*

Walt Whitman (1819–1892): American poet. *Simplicity is the glory of expression! The art of art, the glory of expression and the sunshine of the light of letters, is simplicity.*

Oscar Wilde (1854–1900): Irish writer and poet. *Life is not complex. We are complex. Life is simple, and the simple thing is the right thing.*

Henry Ford (1863–1947): American industrialist. *Nothing is particularly hard if you divide it into small jobs.*

Johann Wolfgang von Goethe (1749–1832): German poet, novelist, and dramatist. *Nothing is true, but that which is simple.*

Sir Thomas More (1478–1535): Lawyer, social philosopher, and author. *The ordinary acts we practice every day at home are of more importance to the soul than their simplicity might suggest.*

Winston Churchill (1874–1965): British politician. *Out of intense complexities intense simplicities emerge.*

Isaac Newton (1643–1727): Scientist. *Nature is pleased with simplicity.*

Eleanor Roosevelt (1884–1962): Former first lady. *A little simplification would be the first step toward rational living, I think.*

Henry David Thoreau (1817–1862): Naturalist, writer, philosopher, poet, abolitionist, surveyor, historian, and leading transcendentalist.

Our life is frittered away by detail.
Simplify, simplify, simplify!
Simplicity of life and elevation of purpose.
In the wildness is the preservation of the world.